Get ready all you crazed followers of Monty Python! Those zany guys with their special brand of humor are at it again.

Continuing in the tradition of universal offensiveness and inexcusable vulgarity they established with *Monty Python's Flying Circus* and *Monty Python and the Holy Grail*, they now bring you the thoroughly uproarious *Life of Brian*. This is a story rivaled in hilarity only by what these manic men have concocted before.

Brian, the boy next door—except that this particular boy was born 1,979 years ago in the land of Judea next door to another nativity scene of considerably greater impact on the future of the world.

This is the FULL script of the major Warner Brothers release.

Monty Python's

THE LIFE
of
BRIAN

(*of Nazareth*)

Written by and Starring

GRAHAM CHAPMAN • JOHN CLEESE
TERRY GILLIAM • ERIC IDLE
TERRY JONES • MICHAEL PALIN

Directed by TERRY JONES • Designed by TERRY GILLIAM

Produced by JOHN GOLDSTONE

Executive Producers
GEORGE HARRISON • DENIS O'BRIEN

ace books
A Division of Charter Communications Inc.
A GROSSET & DUNLAP COMPANY
360 Park Avenue South
New York, New York 10010

MONTY PYTHON'S

THE LIFE OF BRIAN

An ACE Book

This book represents the script in its entirety as it appears in the Grosset & Dunlap edition.

2 4 6 8 0 9 7 5 3
Manufactured in the United States of America

Dramatis Personæ

The Virgin Mandy,
the mother of Brian (A ratbag) .... *Terry Jones*
1st Wise Man .... *Graham Chapman*
2nd Wise Man .... *Michael Palin*
3rd Wise Man .... *John Cleese*
Jesus the Christ .... *Ken Colley*
Brian called Brian .... *Graham Chapman*
Mr. Big Nose .... *Michael Palin*
Mrs. Big Nose .... *Gwen Taylor*
Mr. Cheeky .... *Eric Idle*
Gregory .... *Terence Bayler*
Mrs. Gregory .... *Carol Cleveland*
Man Further Forward .... *Charles McKeown*
Another Person Further Forward .... *Terry Gilliam*
Francis, A Revolutionary .... *Michael Palin*
Reg, Leader of the Judean People's Front ... *John Cleese*
Stan called Loretta, a confused Revolutionary .. *Eric Idle*
Judith, a beautiful Revolutionary ...... *Sue Jones-Davis*
Harry the Haggler, Beard and Stone Salesman . *Eric Idle*
Woman with sick Donkey .... *Gwen Taylor*
Jewish Official at the Stoning .... *John Cleese*
Matthias, a stonee .... *John Young*
Official Stoners Helper .... *Bernard McKenna*
Another Official Stoners Helper ... *Andrew MacLachlan*
Culprit Woman, who casts the first stone ...... *Eric Idle*
Mrs. A., who casts the second stone ..... *Michael Palin*
Ex-Leper .... *Michael Palin*
A weedy Samaritan, at the Forum .... *Neil Innes*
Revolutionaries and Masked Commandos ....
    Terence Bayler, Terry Gilliam, Bernard McKenna,
Chris Langham, Andrew MacLachlan, Charles McKeown

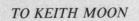

TO KEITH MOON

THE LIFE
of
BRIAN

The Life of Brian
(of Nazareth)

The Night Sky. *Three camels are silhouetted against the bright stars of the moonless sky, moving slowly along the horizon. A star leads them towards* BETHLEHEM.

The WISE MEN *enter the gates of the sleeping town and make their way through the deserted streets. A dog snarls at them. They approach a lighted stable, light streams out. Dismounting and entering they find a typical manger scene, with a baby in a rough crib of straw, patient animals standing around. The mother nods by the side of the child. Suddenly she wakes from her lightish doze, sees them, shrieks and falls backwards off her straw. She's up again in a flash, looking guardedly at them. She is a ratbag.*

MANDY

Who are you?

1ST WISE MAN

We are three wise men.

3RD WISE MAN

We are astrologers. We have come from the East.

MANDY

Is this some kind of joke?

1ST WISE MAN

We wish to praise the infant.

2ND WISE MAN

We must pay homage to him.

MANDY

Homage!! You're all drunk you are. It's
disgusting. Out, out.

3RD WISE MAN

No, no.

MANDY

Coming bursting in here first thing in the morning
with some tale about Oriental fortune tellers . . .
get out.

1ST WISE MAN

No. No, we must see him.

MANDY

Go and praise someone else's brat, go on.

2ND WISE MAN

We were led by a star.

MANDY

Led by a bottle, more like. Get out!

2ND WISE MAN

We must see him. We have brought presents.

MANDY

Out.

1ST WISE MAN

Gold, frankincense, myrrh.

MANDY *changes direction, smooth as silk.*

MANDY

Well, why didn't you say? He's over here . . .
Sorry this place is a bit of a mess. What is myrrh,
anyway?

3RD WISE MAN

It is a valuable balm.

MANDY

A balm, what are you giving him a balm for? It
might bite him.

3RD WISE MAN

What?

MANDY

It's a dangerous animal. Quick, throw it in the
trough.

3RD WISE MAN

No it isn't.

MANDY

Yes it is.

3RD WISE MAN
No, no, it is an ointment.

MANDY
An ointment?

3RD WISE MAN
Look.

MANDY
(sampling the ointment with a grubby finger)
Oh. There is an animal called a balm, or did I dream it? You astrologers, eh? Well, what's he then?

2ND WISE MAN
H'm?

MANDY
What star sign is he?

2ND WISE MAN
Capricorn.

MANDY
Capricorn eh, what are they like?

2ND WISE MAN
He is the son of God, our Messiah.

1ST WISE MAN
King of the Jews.

MANDY
And that's Capricorn, is it?

3RD WISE MAN
No, no, that's just him.

MANDY
Oh, I was going to say, otherwise there'd be a lot of them.

The WISE MEN *are on their knees.*

By what name are you calling him?

Dramatic chord.

MANDY

. . . Brian.

THREE WISE MEN

We worship you, Oh Brian, who are Lord over us all. Praise unto you, Brian and to the Lord our Father. Amen.

MANDY

Do you do a lot of this then?

1ST WISE MAN

What?

MANDY

This praising.

1ST WISE MAN

No, no, no.

MANDY

Oh! Well, if you're dropping by again do pop in.

They take the hint and rise:

And thanks a lot for the gold and frankincense but . . . don't worry too much about the myrrh next time. Thank you. Goodbye.

(to Brian)

Well weren't they nice . . . out of their bloody minds, but still . . .

In the background we see the WISE MEN *pause outside the door as a gentle glow suffuses them. They look at each other, confer and then stride back in and grab the presents off* MANDY *and turn to go again pushing* MANDY *over.*

Here, here, that's mine, you just gave me that.
Ow.

Cut to exterior BETHLEHEM *street again. The* WISE
MEN *come out of the stable bathed in a gentle light.
They look in the direction of the light and we pan to
reveal the archetypal manger scene with* MARY, JOS-
EPH *and the* INFANT JESUS. *The* WISE MEN *move into
shot and kneel.*

Cut back to MANDY *and her brat. It howls.* MANDY
smacks it.

Main title sequence.

MONTY PYTHON'S LIFE OF BRIAN.

The music sweeps—desperately.

Brian . . . the babe they called Brian
Grew . . . grew grew and grew, grew up to be
A boy called Brian
A boy called Brian

He had arms and legs and hands and feet
This boy whose name was Brian
And he grew, grew grew and grew
Grew up to be
Yes he grew up to be
A teenager called Brian
A teenager called Brian
And his face became spotty
Yes his face became spotty
And his voice dropped down low
And things started to grow
On young Brian and show
He was certainly no
No girl named Brian

Not a girl named Brian
And he started to shave
And have one off the wrist
And want to see girls
And go out and get pissed
This man called Brian
This man called Brian

The camera pans slowly across wide open countryside.
Hundreds of people are making their way slowly
towards a distant hillside. We see camels and donkeys
led by swarthy men, some riding, some walking, all
headed beyond our view.

We are up in the hills now, still continuing the pan as
the throng gets larger and picks up a greater sense of
urgency and direction.

Caption: **JUDEA A.D. 33**

2nd Caption: **SATURDAY AFTERNOON.**

3rd Caption: **ABOUT TEA-TIME.**

We hear the distant voice of JESUS CHRIST *floating towards us and cut to see him standing at the summit of a hill. Around him as we track backwards are thousands of people, listening to his words.*

> JESUS
>
> How blest are the sorrowful, for they shall find consolation. How blest are those of gentle spirit. They shall have the earth for their possession. How blest are those who hunger and thirst to see right prevail. They shall be satisfied . . .

CHRIST'S *voice gets fainter as we pull back from him revealing the enormous size of the crowd. Standing*

11

nearby, isolated but alert, is a large contingent of Roman soldiers drawn up in serried ranks, armed, impassive, foreign soldiers on extra-weekend duty, keeping an eye on a large and potentially anti-Roman crowd.

We are a long way back from JESUS *now, on another hillside towards the back of this huge multitude, his voice is barely audible on the wind. People are straining to hear. The camera comes to rest by* MANDY, *older now by thirty three years, but still a ratbag.*

MANDY

Speak up!

BRIAN

Mum! Sh!

MANDY

Well I can't hear a thing! Let's go to the stoning.

BIG NOSE

Sh!

BRIAN

You can go to a stoning any time.

MANDY

Oh, come on Brian!

BIG NOSE

Will you be quiet?

WIFE

Don't pick you nose.

BIG NOSE

I wasn't picking my nose . . . I was scratching.

WIFE

You were picking it while you were talking to that lady.

BIG NOSE

I wasn't.

Leave it alone . . . give it a rest . . .

MR. CHEEKY

Do you mind . . . I can't hear a word he's saying.

WIFE

Don't you "do you mind" me . . . I'm talking to my husband.

MR. CHEEKY

Well go and talk to him somewhere else! I can't hear a bloody thing!

BIG NOSE

Don't you swear at my wife.

MR. CHEEKY

I was only asking her to shut up so we can hear what he's saying, big nose.

WIFE

Don't you call my husband "big nose."

MR. CHEEKY

Well he has got a big nose.

Suddenly another rather well-heeled Jew in a toga turns around. He constantly has trouble with his toga and has to keep pushing it back in place. His voice is very cultured. A small boy holds a large parasol over his head. His name is GREGORY *and he is out for the day with his wife.*

GREGORY

Could you be quiet, please?
(to Mr. Cheeky)
What was that?

MR. CHEEKY

I don't know. . . . I was too busy talking to big nose.

I think it was "Blessed are the Cheesemakers."

WIFE OF GREGORY

What's so special about the cheesemakers?

GREGORY

It's not meant to be taken literally. Obviously it refers to any manufacturers of dairy products.

MR. CHEEKY

(to Big Nose)
See—if you hadn't been going on, you'd have heard that, Big Nose.

BIG NOSE

Hey, if you say that once more, I'll smash your fucking face in.

MR. CHEEKY

Better keep listening . . . might be a bit about "Blessed are the big noses."

BRIAN

Oh lay off him.

MR. CHEEKY

(rounding on Brian)
You're not so bad yourself, Conkface. Where are you two from? Nose City?

BIG NOSE

Listen! I said one more time . . . mate and I'll take you to the fucking cleaners.

WIFE

Language! And don't pick your nose!

BIG NOSE

I wasn't going to pick my nose. I was going to thump him.

ANOTHER PERSON

I think it was "Blessed are the Greek."

14

GREGORY

<u>The</u> Greek?

ANOTHER PERSON

Apparently he's going to inherit the earth.

GREGORY

Did anyone catch his name?

BIG NOSE

I'll thump him if he calls me Big Nose again.

MR. CHEEKY

Oh shut up, Big Nose.

BIG NOSE

Oooh! Right I warned you . . . I really will slug you so hard . . .

WIFE

Oh it's the Meek . . . Blessed are the meek! That's nice, I'm glad they're getting something 'cos they have a hell of a time.

MR. CHEEKY

Listen . . . I'm only telling the truth . . . you have got a very big nose.

BIG NOSE

(trying desperately to control his anger)
Your nose is going to be three foot wide across your face when I've finished with you.

MR. CHEEKY

Who hit yours then? Goliath's big brother?

BIG NOSE

Ooooh . . . oohh . . . aargh . . . ah
(supreme self-control)
That's your last warning . . .

MRS. GREGORY

Oh do pipe d . . .

BIG NOSE *lets fly an almighty punch and hits* MRS.

GREGORY *hard in the face. Horrible crunching of fist on bone.*

A general scuffle breaks out.

> ### BIG NOSE
> Silly bitch, getting in the way.

> ### MANDY
> Brian! Come on, let's go to the stoning.

> ### BRIAN
> Alright.

MANDY *starts to move off,* BRIAN *reluctantly follows.* ROMAN SOLDIERS *start to move in to separate the combatants.*

At this point we see that BRIAN *has his eye on a rather attractive young woman who is part of a group of three intense young men whose dress sets them apart from the rest.*

They are starting to leave as well.

As BRIAN *follows his mother, he edges round the group gazing at the girl.*

We catch the following conversation.

> ### FRANCIS
> Well, Blessed is just about everyone with a vested interest in the status quo, as far as I can tell, Reg.

> ### REG
> What Jesus blatantly fails to appreciate is that it is the Meek who are the problem.

> ### JUDITH
> *(the girl* BRIAN *has been admiring)*
> Yes . . . yes . . . I see . . .

JUDITH *catches sight of* BRIAN *gazing at her, and* BRIAN *hastily drops his eyes, at the same moment,* MANDY *turns.*

MANDY

Come on Brian or they'll have stoned him before
we get there.

BRIAN *hurries off, involuntarily fingering his nose.*

BRIAN

Alright, Mum.

Cut to MANDY *and* BRIAN *walking along towards the
city, amongst some date palms,* MANDY *is fiddling
away putting on a very obvious false beard.*

MANDY

Oh I hate these things.

BRIAN

Why aren't women allowed to go to stonings,
Mum?

MANDY

Because it's written, that's why.

They are approaching the stall of HARRY, *the stone
salesman. He has various sizes of rocks and stones,
graded and displayed for sale. Little packets of gravel
are piled in cone twists. An elderly woman, almost bent
double by the weight of a huge donkey on her shoul-
ders, staggers past. The stone salesman whips open his
coat, revealing rows of artificial beards displayed in
the lining.*

HARRY

Psst! Beard, madam?

DONKEY WOMAN

Look, I haven't got time to go to stonings—
(referring to donkey)
He's not well again.

The SALESMAN *turns to* BRIAN *and* MANDY.

17

HARRY

(to Mandy)

Want a few stones, sir?

MANDY

No thank you. They've got a lot up there, lying around on the ground.

HARRY

Not like these, sir . . .

(showing one)

Look at that—feel the quality of this—that's craftsmanship, sir.

MANDY *stops and appraises the stone. Weighs one up professionally.*

MANDY

Alright, we'll have two with points and a big flat one.

18

BRIAN
Can I have a flat one, Mum?

MANDY
Ssh!

BRIAN
Oh sorry . . . Dad.

MANDY
(adopting a lower register)
Alright, two points, two flats, and a packet of gravel.

HARRY
Packet of gravel. Should be a good one this afternoon, local boy.

MANDY
Oh good.

The Stoning Place. An OFFICIAL *stands there, with some helpers, confronting the potential stonee,* MAT-THIAS. *A large crowd watches. 90% are women in beards. Around the perimeter are a few Roman troops.*

JEWISH OFFICIAL
Matthias son of Deuteronomy of Gath . . .

MATTHIAS
(to Official's Helper)
Do I say "Yes"?

OFFICIAL'S HELPER
Yes.

MATTHIAS
Yes.

OFFICIAL
You have been found guilty by the elders of the town of uttering the name of our Lord and so as a blasphemer you are to be stoned to death.

MATTHIAS

Look, I'd had a lovely supper and all I said to my wife was, ''That piece of halibut was good enough for Jehovah.''

OFFICIAL

Blasphemy! He's said it again.

WOMEN

Yes, he did.

OFFICIAL

Did you hear him?

WOMEN

Yes we did. Really.

OFFICIAL

Are there any women here today?

20

The WOMEN *all shake their heads. The* OFFICIAL *faces* MATTHIAS *again.*

OFFICIAL
Very well, by virtue of the authority vested in me . . .

One of the WOMEN *throws a stone and it hits* MATTHIAS *on the knee.*

MATTHIAS
Ow. Lay off. We haven't started yet.

OFFICIAL
(turning around)
Come on, who threw that?

Silence.

Who threw that stone? Come on.

Some of the WOMEN *point to the culprit.*

WOMEN
She did.
He did.
He.
Him.

During this they keep their voices as low as they can, in pitch but not in volume.

CULPRIT
(very deep voice)
Sorry, I thought we'd started.

OFFICIAL
Go to the back.

CULPRIT
(disappointed)
Oh dear.
(goes to back)

OFFICIAL

There's always one, isn't there? Now, where were we? . . .

MATTHIAS

Look. I don't think it ought to be blasphemy, just saying Jehovah!

Sensation!!!!! The WOMEN *gasp.*

WOMEN

(high voices)
He said it again.
(low voices)
He said it again.

OFFICIAL

(to Matthias)
You're only making it worse for yourself.

22

MATTHIAS

Making it worse? How can it be worse? Jehovah, Jehovah, Jehovah.

Greater Sensation!!!!!

OFFICIAL

I'm warning you. If you say Jehovah once more . . .
(he gasps at his error and claps his hand over his mouth)

A stone hits him on the side of the head. He reacts.

OFFICIAL

Right! Who threw that?

WOMEN

(high voices)
It was her. It was <u>him.</u>
(low voices)
It was him.

OFFICIAL

Was it you?

MRS. A

Yes.

OFFICIAL

Alright.

MRS. A

Well, you did say Jehovah.

WOMEN *all shriek and throw stones at her from very close range. She falls to the ground stunned. Quick cut of* ROMANS *reacting. They shake their heads and mutter to each other.*

OFFICIAL

Stop that. Stop it, will you stop that. Now look, no-one is to stone anyone until I blow this whistle.

<u>Even</u> . . . and I want to make this absolutely
clear . . . <u>even</u> if they <u>do</u> say Jehovah.

There is a pause. Then all the WOMEN *throw stones at
the* OFFICIAL *and he goes down in a heap. Five* WOMEN
carry a huge rock, run up and drop it on the OFFICIAL.
Everyone claps. The GUARDS *sadly shake their heads.*

JERUSALEM, *outside the city gate. An enormous statue
of* PILATE *is being dragged along by ox-cart.* PEOPLE
*are coming and going through the main gate. Near us
are some old crosses with one or two twisted skeletons
hanging on them. This is a common sight—no one pays
any attention to them.* BRIAN *and* MANDY *are making
their way beside the huge high walls of the city.*

BRIAN

<u>Have</u> I got a big nose, Mum?

24

MANDY

Oh, <u>stop</u> thinking about SEX!

BRIAN

I wasn't.

MANDY

You're always on about it! Morning noon and night! Will the girls like this? Will the girls like that? Is it too big? Is it too small?

BRIAN

I was just wondering if you thought my nose . . .

MANDY

Get your filthy little mind off it! You're 30 years old, you should have grown out of all that!

BRIAN

I'm only just starting to get interested in it, Mum.

MANDY

It's time you got interested in a job, my lad!

As they pass through the city gate, they attract a rather muscular, fit and healthy young BEGGAR, *who pursues them relentlessly through the busy streets.*

EX-LEPER

Spare a talent for an old ex-leper, sir.

MANDY

(to ex-leper)
Buzz off!

The EX-LEPER *has come round to* BRIAN'S *side.*

EX-LEPER

(to Brian)
Spare a talent for an old ex-leper, sir.

BRIAN

Did you say—ex-leper?

EX-LEPER

That's right, sir.
(he salutes)
. . . sixteen years behind the bell, and proud of it, thank you sir.

BRIAN

What happened?

EX-LEPER

I was cured, sir.

BRIAN

Cured?

EX-LEPER

Yes sir, a bloody miracle, sir. Bless you.

BRIAN

Who cured you?

EX-LEPER

Jesus did. I was hopping along, when suddenly he comes and cures me. One minute I'm a leper with a trade, next moment me livelihood's gone. Not so much as a by your leave.
(gestures in the manner of a conjuror)
You're cured mate, sod you.

MANDY

Go away.

EX-LEPER

Look. I'm not saying that being a leper was a bowl of cherries. But it was a living. I mean, you try waving muscular suntanned limbs in people's faces demanding compassion. It's a bloody disaster.

BRIAN

You could go and get yourself a decent job, couldn't you?

EX-LEPER

Look, sir, my family has been in begging six generations. I'm not about to become a goat-herd, just because some long-haired conjuror starts mucking about.
(makes gesture again)
Just like that. "You're cured." Bloody do-gooder!

BRIAN

Well, why don't you go and tell him you want to be a leper again?

EX-LEPER

Ah yeah, I could do that, sir, yes, I suppose I

could. What I was going to do was ask him if he could . . . you know, just make me a bit lame in one leg during the week, you know, something beggable, but not leprosy, which is a pain in the arse to be quite blunt, sir, excuse my French but . . .

They have reached BRIAN *and* MANDY'S *house.* MANDY *goes in.*

BRIAN *gives the* BEGGAR *a coin.*

BRIAN

There you are.

EX-LEPER

Thank you sir . . . half a denari for my bloody life story!

There's no pleasing some people.

EX-LEPER

That's just what Jesus said.

BRIAN *turns and goes indoors.*

Inside MANDY'S HOUSE. MANDY *enters. The room is very austere. Sparsely furnished. On the only chair a large, thick-set* CENTURION *is seated rather uncomfortably. He looks slightly ill-at-ease.*

MANDY

'urry up Brian. Oh!

The CENTURION *half rises as* MANDY *enters.*

CENTURION

Good afternoon.

MANDY

Oh hello, Officer . . . I'll be with you in a few moments, alright, dear?

BRIAN

(whispering to Mandy)
What's <u>he</u> doing here?

MANDY

Now don't start that! Brian, go and do your room.

BRIAN

Bloody Romans!

MANDY

(still whispering)
Now look, if it wasn't for them,

She gestures at the CENTURION, *who starts polishing his uniform with great application.*

we wouldn't have all this, and don't you forget it.
(she nods at empty room)

29

BRIAN

Oh Mother, we don't owe the Romans anything.

MANDY

Well that's not entirely true, Brian.

BRIAN

What do you mean?

MANDY *looks towards* ROMAN, *who is still fiddling with his gear and trying to make himself look inconspicuous. She turns back to* BRIAN *and takes him on one side.*

MANDY

(sotto voce)
Well . . . you know you were asking me about your . . . er . . .

BRIAN

My nose?

MANDY

Yes . . . well there's a reason why it's . . . like it is . . . Brian.

BRIAN

What is it?

MANDY

I know I should have told you long ago, but I . . . well, Brian . . . your father isn't Mr. Cohen.

BRIAN

I never thought he was.

MANDY

None of your cheek! He was a Roman, Brian.
Dramatic chord.

He was a centurion . . . in the Roman army.

BRIAN *looks stunned. His hand involuntarily goes to his nose.*

BRIAN

You mean . . . you were raped?

MANDY

Well at first . . . yes . . .

BRIAN

Who was it?

MANDY

Nortius Maximus his name was . . . promised me the known world he did . . . I was to be taken to Rome . . . House by the Forum . . . slaves . . . asses' milk . . . as much gold as I could eat . . . then—he, having his way with me had, voom! Like a rat out of an aqueduct.

BRIAN

The bastard.

MANDY

I went down the barracks a couple of months later . . . Could I have a word with Nortius Maximus? I said. Nortius Maximus? They said—you've been had, Missus . . . you've been had.

BRIAN

Typical . . .

MANDY

(*quickly*)
So next time you go on about the "bloody Romans," don't forget you're one of them, Brian.

BRIAN

I'm not a Roman, Mum and I never will be! I'm a Kike! A Yid! A Hebe! A Hook-nose! I'm Kosher, Mum. I'm a Red Sea Pedestrian and proud of it!

BRIAN *storms out and slams the door.*

MANDY *looks long-sufferingly over at the* CENTURION.

> MANDY
> Sex sex sex—that's all they think about.

She moves towards the CENTURION.

A huge Roman amphitheatre *sparsely attended. There is a large group of* ROMANS, *but hardly any crowd. A fight has just ended and a couple of* OLD LADIES *are busy cleaning up . . . putting limbs into their baskets. Occasionally one finds a hand with a ring or two on it, which she stuffs into her robe.*

BRIAN *comes into shot. He has a tray round his neck and is selling tit-bits.*

> BRIAN
> Larks' tongues . . . Wrens' livers . . .
> Chaffinch brains . . .

As he's looking around to sell his wares, he suddenly catches sight of JUDITH *on the other side of the amphitheatre. She is with the other* REVOLUTIONARIES *and is earnestly talking to them.* BRIAN *starts making his way round towards her.*

BRIAN

(with spirit)
Jaguar's earlobes!

Cut to the REVOLUTIONARIES—REG, FRANCIS, STAN *and* JUDITH *seated in the stands. They speak conspiratorially.*

JUDITH

. . . Any Anti-Imperialist group like ours must <u>reflect</u> such a divergence of interests within its powerbase.

REG

Agreed.

General nodding.
Francis?

FRANCIS

I think Judith's point of view is valid here, Reg, provided the Movement never forgets that it is the unalienable right of every man . . .

STAN

Or woman.

FRANCIS

Or woman . . . to rid himself . . .

STAN

Or herself.

REG

Or herself. Agreed. Thank you, brother.

STAN

Or sister.

FRANCIS

Thank you, brother. Or sister. Where was I?

REG

I thought you'd finished.

FRANCIS

Oh did I? Right.

REG

Furthermore, it is the birthright of every
man . . .

STAN

Or woman.

REG

Why don't you shut up about women, Stan,
you're putting us off.

STAN

Women have a perfect right to play a part in our
movement, Reg.

FRANCIS

Why are you always on about women, Stan?

STAN

. . . I want to be one.

REG

. . . What?

STAN

I want to be a woman. From now on I want you all
to call me Loretta.

REG

What!?

STAN

It's my right as a man.

JUDITH

Why do you want to be Loretta, Stan?

STAN

I want to have babies.

REG

You want to have babies????!!!

STAN

It's every man's right to have babies if he wants them.

REG

But you can't have babies.

STAN

Don't you oppress me.

REG

I'm not oppressing you, Stan—you haven't got a womb. Where's the foetus going to gestate? You going to keep it in a box?

STAN *starts crying.*

JUDITH

Here! I've got an idea. Suppose you agree that he can't actually have babies, not having a womb, which is nobody's fault, not even the Romans, but that he can have the right to have babies.

FRANCIS

Good idea, Judith. We shall fight the oppressors for your right to have babies, brother. Sister, sorry.

REG

What's the point?

FRANCIS

What?

REG

What's the point of fighting for his right to have babies, when he can't have babies?

35

It is symbolic of our struggle against oppression.

It's symbolic of his struggle against reality.

Trumpets. A fanfare. A SAMARITAN *is pushed out into the arena.*

There is a small spattering of applause from the sparse CROWD. *The atmosphere resembles the second day of a mid-week cricket match between Northamptonshire and the minor counties at Kettering.*

The SAMARITAN *runs back through the gate again. The* CROWD *laughs. The* SAMARITAN *reappears, being pushed into the arena, and the door behind him is slammed closed. A huge* GLADIATOR *advances on him. The* SAMARITAN *takes one look at the* GLADIATOR *and sets off at full speed round the perimeter of the arena. The* GLADIATOR *lumbers after him. After a few seconds it becomes apparent that the* SAMARITAN *is going to take a lot of catching. The* CROWD *is disgruntled and a ragged chant starts:* "What a load of rubbish." *Some slow handclapping.*

By this time BRIAN *has worked his way around to a point near the* REVOLUTIONARIES.

BRIAN
Larks' tongues . . . otters' noses . . . Ocelot spleens.

REG *looks up and calls to* BRIAN.

REG
You got any nuts?

BRIAN
I haven't got any nuts, sorry, I've got wrens' livers, badgers' spleens . . .

REG

No, no, no.

BRIAN

Otters' noses.

REG

No. I don't want any of that Roman rubbish.

JUDITH

Why don't you sell proper food?

BRIAN

Proper food?

REG

Yeah, not those rich imperialist tit-bits.

BRIAN

Don't blame me—I didn't <u>ask</u> to sell this stuff.

37

REG

Alright . . . bag of otters' noses.

BRIAN

(reluctant to move away)
Are you the . . . Judean Peoples' Front?

REG *hears this and leans across.*

REG

Fuck off!

BRIAN

. . . What?

REG

(incredulously)
Judean Peoples' Front!??? We're the Peoples' Front of Judea.

BRIAN *looks blank.*

38

REG
(scornfully to the others)
Fucking Judean Peoples' Front! Huh!

Scornful laughter.

FRANCIS
Wankers.

REG
(to Brian, fiercely)
The Peoples' Front of Judea fucking gets things <u>done</u>!

BRIAN
Oh!

REG
We're not a load of fucking <u>splitters</u>!

ALL
<u>Splitters</u>!! Fucking splitters!!

REG
Huh! Fucking Judean . . . fucking Peoples' fucking Front.

BRIAN
. . . Which are you again?

REG
We're the Peoples' Front of fucking Judea.

BRIAN
(tentatively to Judith)
Can I . . . join your group?

REG
No. Piss off.

BRIAN
(referring to tray)
I don't want to sell this stuff you know . . . it's only a job. I hate the Romans as much as anybody.

Sh!

The REVOLUTIONARIES *all look around anxiously to make sure no one has heard.*

REG

Listen. The only people we hate <u>more</u> than the Romans . . . are the fucking Judean Peoples' Front.

ALL

Splitters! Bastards!

FRANCIS

<u>And</u> the Judean Popular People's Front.

ALL

Yeah, splitters!

STAN

And the Peoples' Front of Judea.

ALL

Yeah.

REG

What?

STAN

The Peoples' Front of Judea! Splitters!

REG

<u>We're</u> the Peoples' Front of Judea.

STAN

Oh. Are we? I thought . . . we were the Popular Front.

REG

Peoples' Front. Twit.

FRANCIS

Whatever happened to the Popular Front, Reg?

He's over there.

Splitter!

REG *turns to* BRIAN.

REG
What's your name?

BRIAN
Brian . . . er . . . Brian Cohen.

REG
We may have a little job for you, Brian.

Darkened streets. Night time. *Figures flit from shadow to shadow.* PILATE'S *palace looms over the deserted square.* BRIAN *totters into view, and stands there uncertainly for a moment, then makes for the high wall of the Roman palace. When he reaches the foot of the high wall he starts painting on it in pathetically small letters—"Romanes Eunt Domus." As he writes, a* CENTURION *with a couple of* SOLDIERS *approach him stealthily. Suddenly a hand lands on* BRIAN'S *shoulder.*

CENTURION
What's this then? "Romanes Eunt Domus"?
People called Romanes, they go the house.

BRIAN
(defiantly)
It says "Romans go home."

CENTURION
No it doesn't. What's Latin for Romans?
(slaps him)
Come on . . . come on . . .

BRIAN
Romanus!

Goes like?

BRIAN

Er . . . annus.

CENTURION

Vocative plural of annus is . . .
(tweaking Brian's hair)

BRIAN

Anni.

CENTURION

Romani . . .
(crossing out Es and substituting I, flaps Brian)
"Eunt"? What's "eunt"?

BRIAN

Go . . .
(he is shaken)
. . . Er . . .

CENTURION

Conjugate the verb to go.

BRIAN

Ire . . . eo . . . is . . . it . . . imus . . . itis
. . . eunt . . .

CENTURION

So eunt is . . ?

BRIAN

Third person plural present indicative. They go.

CENTURION

But, 'Romans go home' is an order . . . so you
must use . . .

BRIAN

The imperative!!

CENTURION

Which is . . ?

BRIAN

Aaah . . . i . . .

CENTURION

How many Romans?

BRIAN

Plural! Plural! Ite!! Ite!!

CENTURION

Ite . . .
(*changes it*)
Domus . . . what is domus?

BRIAN

Er . . .

CENTURION

Romans go home. This is motion towards, isn't it
boy?

BRIAN

Dative, sir.

CENTURION

(*drawing his sword and holding it to Brian's
throat*)
Dative!

BRIAN

No, no dative . . .

CENTURION

. . . What?

BRIAN

Er . . . accusative . . . er . . . domum . . . ad
domum, sir.

CENTURION

Except that domus takes the . . ?

BRIAN

. . . Oh, the locative . . . sir!

43

Which is . . .

BRIAN

Domum?

CENTURION

So we have . . . Romani, ite domum. Do you understand?

BRIAN

Yes, sir.

CENTURION

Now write it out a hundred times.

BRIAN

Yes sir, hail Caesar, sir.

CENTURION

Hail Caesar.

BRIAN

Yes sir.

CENTURION

And if it isn't done by sunrise, I'll cut your balls off.

BRIAN

Thank you sir. Hail Caesar, sir and everything, sir.

(he starts writing it out)

Fade down, *as the* CENTURION *goes, leaving the* SOL-DIERS *behind to enforce the punishment. Fade up again. Morning.*

By use of a ladder, BRIAN *has virtually covered the huge wall with 'Romani ite domum.' He finishes the 100th line. The* TWO ROMANS *are in the background.* BRIAN *calls out.*

BRIAN

Finished.

Right. Now don't do it again.

The interior of MATTHIA'S HOUSE. *A cellar-like room with a very conspiratorial atmosphere.*

REG *and* STAN *are seated at a table at one end of the room.* FRANCIS, *dressed in commando gear—black robes and a red sash around his head, is standing by a plan on the wall. He is addressing an audience of about eight* MASKED COMMANDOS. *Their faces are partially hidden.*

FRANCIS
We get in through the underground heating system here . . . up through to the main audience chamber here . . . and Pilate's Wife's bedroom is here. Having grabbed his wife, we inform Pilate that she is in our custody and forthwith issue our demands. Any questions?

COMMANDO XERXES
What exactly are the demands?

REG
We're giving Pilate two days to dismantle the entire apparatus of the Roman Imperialist State and if he doesn't agree immediately we execute her.

MATTHIAS
Cut her head off?

FRANCIS
Cut all her bits off, send 'em back every hour on the hour . . . show him we're not to be trifled with.

REG
Also, we're demanding a ten-foot mahogany statue of the Emperor Julius Caesar with his cock hanging out.

What? They'll never agree to that, Reg.

REG

That's just a bargaining counter. And of course, we point out that they bear full responsibility when we chop her up, <u>and</u> . . . that we shall <u>not</u> submit to blackmail.

Applause.

ALL

No blackmail!!!!

REG

They've bled us white, the bastards. They've taken everything we had, not just from us, from our fathers and from our fathers' fathers.

STAN

And from our fathers' fathers' fathers.

REG

Yes.

STAN

And our fathers' fathers' fathers' fathers.

REG

Alright, Stan. Don't labour the point. And what have they ever given us <u>in return</u>?

He pauses smugly.

Voice from masked COMMANDO.

XERXES

The aqueduct?

REG

What?

XERXES

The aqueduct.

REG

Oh yeah, yeah they gave us that. Yeah. That's true.

MASKED COMMANDO

And the sanitation!

STAN

Oh yes . . . sanitation, Reg, you remember what the city used to be like.

Murmurs of agreement.

REG

Alright, I'll grant you that the aqueduct and the sanitation are two things that the Romans <u>have</u> done . . .

MATTHIAS

And the roads . . .

REG

(sharply)

Well <u>yes obviously</u> the roads . . . the roads go without saying. But apart from the aqueduct, the sanitation and the roads . . .

ANOTHER MASKED COMMANDO

Irrigation . . .

OTHER MASKED VOICES

Medicine . . . Education . . . Health.

REG

Yes . . . alright, fair enough . . .

COMMANDO NEARER THE FRONT

And the wine . . .

GENERAL

Oh yes! True!

FRANCIS

Yeah. That's something we'd really miss if the Romans left, Reg.

Public baths!

STAN
And it's safe to walk in the streets at night now.

FRANCIS
Yes, they certainly know how to keep order . . .

General nodding.

. . . let's face it, they're the only ones who could in a place like this.

More general murmurs of agreement.

REG
Alright . . . alright . . . but apart from better sanitation and medicine and education and irrigation and public health and roads and a freshwater system and baths and public order . . . what have the Romans done for us . . . ?

XERXES
Brought peace!

REG
(very angry, he's not having a good meeting at all)
What!? Oh . . .
(scornfully)
Peace, yes . . . shut up!

There is a knock on the door. Instantly everyone leaps into various ill-concealed hiding places. MATTHIAS *snaps into an old-man routine, looks round to check everyone is badly hidden, then opens the door.*

MATTHIAS
I'm a poor man, my sight is poor, my legs are old and bent . . .

JUDITH
It's alright, Matthias.

MATTHIAS
(back into the room at large)
It's all clear.

The room fills up again as people reappear from their several hiding places. Except REG who has to be collected by FRANCIS from under the table.

FRANCIS
Reg! It's alright it's Judith.

REG
(as he reappears)
What went wrong?

JUDITH
The first blow has been struck, Reg.
(her eyes are afire with revolutionary zeal)

REG
D'you finish the slogan?

JUDITH
A hundred times! In letters 10 feet high! All the way round the palace!

A buzz of excitement.

REG
(desperately unenthusiastic)
Oh great . . . !

He flashes a brief look of alarm at FRANCIS, then returns to his revolutionary authority.

Well . . . we need do-ers in our movement, Brian. But before you join us know this: there is not one of us here who would not gladly suffer death to rid this country of the Romans once and for all.

VOICE FROM BACK
Well, one!

Oh yeah. There is one . . . but otherwise we're solid. Are you with us?

BRIAN

Yes!
(He raises his arm in the revolutionary salute.)

REG

From now on you shall be called Brian that is called Brian.

Wide shot exterior of PILATE'S *palace. Night time. Many* ROMANS *are attempting to scrub off* BRIAN'S *slogans by torchlight. Unseen figures flit past, hugging the darkness. A grate is raised and muffled black-robed figures drop into the hole below.* BRIAN *is the last one to drop down.* REG *replaces the iron grating over his head.* BRIAN *looks up through the grating.*

BRIAN

Aren't you coming with us to . . .

REG

(making revolutionary gesture)
Solidarity, Brother.

REG *hurries away.*

BRIAN

Oh yes . . . solidarity, Reg.

The REVOLUTIONARIES *make their way through the drainage tunnel, and enter the main hypocaust or central heating duct that lies underneath* PILATE'S *audience chamber.*

Directly above their heads, on the floor of PILATE'S AUDIENCE CHAMBER, *is a large rather erotic mosaic, in which a naked couple are embracing. The man wears a fig leaf.*

Suddenly the fig leaf rises up and FRANCIS'S *face appears underneath it. He looks about and then climbs out into the room. The others follow.*

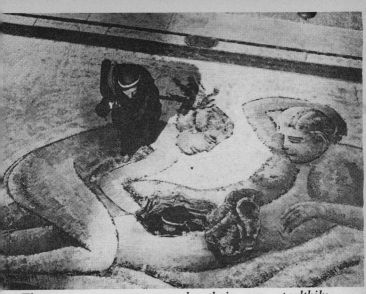

The REVOLUTIONARIES *make their way stealthily through the slumbering palace, eventually reaching a corridor which leads to* PILATE'S WIFE'S *bedroom. They see the door in the distance, and nod to each other silently. The coast is clear. They begin slowly moving forward. As they near the door an* IDENTICAL GROUP *appears from round the corner and makes for the door too.*

There is a moment's pause as they look at each other.

The OTHER GROUP *are dressed pretty much the same except that they wear a yellow head band instead of red.*

There is a rather embarrassed pause, while the TWO GROUPS *look at each other. The* LEADER *of the* OTHER REVOLUTIONARIES *is called* DEADLY DIRK*.*

(saluting)
Campaign for Free Galilee.

FRANCIS

Oh . . . er . . . Peoples' Front of Judea . . .
Officials.

Another pause.

FRANCIS

(trying to sound nonchalant)
What er . . . are you doing here?

DEADLY DIRK

(with enthusiasm)
We're going to kidnap Pilate's Wife . . . take her
back . . . issue demands.

FRANCIS

What? That's our plan.

DEADLY DIRK

Well we were here first.

FRANCIS

What do you mean?

DEADLY DIRK

We thought of it first.

WARRIS

Oh yes?

DEADLY DIRK

Yes, a couple of years ago.

COMMANDOS

Ha ha.

FRANCIS

You got all your demands worked out then?

DEADLY DIRK

Course we have.

FRANCIS

What are they then?

DEADLY DIRK

We're not telling <u>you.</u>

FRANCIS & OTHERS

Ah ha ha ha.

DEADLY DIRK

We thought of it before you anyway.

WARRIS

Did not.

DEADLY DIRK

We bloody did.

FRANCIS

Didn't.

BRIAN

Ssh!

OTHERS

Ssssssh!

DEADLY DIRK

We've been planning this for months.

FRANCIS

Tough titty for you, fish face.

DEADLY DIRK *pokes* FRANCIS *in the eye. Instantly a fight breaks out.*

BRIAN

Brothers, we should be struggling together!

FRANCIS

(between gritted teeth)
We are.

BRIAN

Brothers! We mustn't fight with each other.

Surely we should be united against the common enemy.

Both REVOLUTIONARY GROUPS *in horrified unison:*

ALL

The Judean Peoples Front?????

BRIAN

No no, the Romans.

ALL

Oh! Yes, yes.

FRANCIS

He's right. Let's go in and get her out, and we can argue afterwards.

OTHERS

Alright . . . alright . . . solidarity.

They move towards the heavy door.

Inside the bedroom it is very dark, but they can just make out the silhouette of PILATE'S WIFE'S *bed. They creep towards it. Her slumbering form is snoring gently. Suddenly they fling the net over her and leap upon her. There is a brief intense struggle on the bed. Then inexorably the huge mass of* PILATE'S WIFE *rises from the bed like some Leviathan arising from the Plutonic depths.*

The REVOLUTIONARIES *are clinging onto her, some round her legs, some on her arms and one or two round her neck. With amazing strength she makes her way to the door, still carrying one with her. Then she speeds off down the corridor and round the corner. The* REVOLUTIONARIES *give chase.*

Round the corner she nips into an alcove, one REVOLUTIONARY *clinging to her neck is crushed against the wall, and winded. The* OTHER REVOLUTIONARIES *thunder past.*

PILATE'S WIFE *steps out of the shadows. The* WINDED
REVOLUTIONARY *round her neck is able to get his
breath, and with a cry he falls to the floor.*

His cry attracts the others, who turn and see PILATE'S
WIFE *disappearing towards her room again. They give
chase, but she is too far ahead and gains her bedroom
first. She slams the door and locks it.*

The rest of the REVOLUTIONARIES *arrive and rattle the
door handle.*

FRANCIS

Shit!

WARRIS

I don't believe it!

*It looks as if a fight is about to break out when suddenly
the door opens and the last battered* REVOLUTIONARY

is thrown out on his ear. The door slams again and locks.

Too late FRANCIS *leaps for the door and tries it. He turns on* DEADLY DIRK *with contempt.*

FRANCIS

You stupid bastard.

DEADLY DIRK *punches* FRANCIS *in the face.* FRANCIS *goes out like a light. A fight breaks out. The fight is desperate and violent.*

A couple of ROMAN GUARDS *approach and watch as the two* REVOLUTIONARY GROUPS *proceed to wipe each other out.* BRIAN *rushes around desperately but unavailingly attempting to stop the senseless slaughter. The* ROMANS *watch curiously but make no attempt to interfere.* FRANCIS *seizes his chance and runs away. Eventually only* BRIAN *is left standing. Around him lie the remains of the two* REVOLUTIONARY GROUPS. *He looks up and notices the* ROMANS *for the first time. They draw their swords and approach him.* BRIAN *prepares to defend himself, but just behind him the door swings ominously open and the huge figure of* PILATE'S WIFE *appears over his shoulder. Her vast fist descends on* BRIAN'S *head and he drops straight into unconsciousness.*

He wakes up with a smile on his face to find himself being dragged along a cell corridor by TWO GUARDS. *The horrible figure of the* JAILER *spits at him and flings him into a dark damp cell, slamming the iron grate behind him and turning the key hollowly in the lock.* BRIAN *slumps to the floor. A voice comes out of the darkness behind him.*

BEN

You <u>lucky</u> bastard!

BRIAN *spins round and peers into the gloom.*

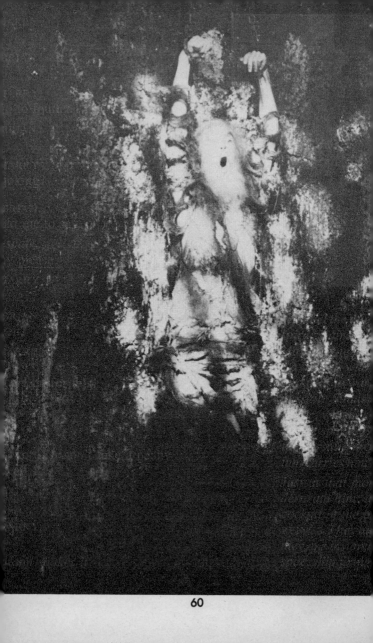

Who's that?

In the darkness BRIAN *just makes out an emaciated figure, suspended on the wall, with his feet off the ground, by chains round his wrists. This is* BEN.

BEN

You lucky, lucky bastard.

BRIAN

What?

BEN

(with great bitterness)
Proper little gaoler's pet, aren't we?

BRIAN

(ruffled)
What do you mean?

BEN

You must have slipped him a few shekels, eh!

BRIAN

Slipped him a few shekels! You saw him spit in my face!

BEN

Ohhh! What wouldn't I give to be spat at in the face! I sometimes hang awake at nights dreaming of being spat at in the face.

BRIAN

Well, it's not exactly friendly, is it? They had me in manacles.

BEN

Manacles! Oooh.
(his eyes go quite dreamy)
My idea of heaven is to be allowed to be put in manacles . . . just for a few hours. They must think the sun shines out of your arse, sonny!

BRIAN

Listen! They beat me up before they threw me in here.

BEN

Oh yeah? The only day they don't beat me up is on my birthday.

BRIAN

Oh shut up.

BEN

Well, your type makes me sick! You come in here, you get treated like Royalty, and everyone outside thinks you're a bloody martyr.

BRIAN

Oh, lay off me . . . I've had a hard time!

BEN

<u>You've</u> had a hard time! Listen, sonny! I've been here five years and they only hung me the right way up yesterday!

BRIAN

Alright! Alright!

BEN

I just wish I had half your luck. They must think you're Lord God Almighty!

BRIAN

What'll they do to me?

BEN

Oh, you'll probably get away with crucifixion.

BRIAN

Crucifixion!

BEN

Yeah, first offence.

BRIAN

Get away with crucifixion!

BEN

Best thing the Romans ever did for us.

BRIAN

(incredulous)
What?

BEN

Oh yeah. If we didn't have crucifixion this
country would be in a right bloody mess I tell you.

BRIAN

(who can stand it no longer)
Guard!

BEN

Nail 'em up I say!

BRIAN

(dragging himself over to the door)
Guard!

BEN

Nail some sense into them!

GUARD

(looking through the bars)
What do you want?

BRIAN

I want to be moved to another cell.

GUARD *spits in his face.*

BRIAN

Oh!
(he recoils in helpless disgust)

BEN

Oh . . . look at that! Bloody favouritism!

GUARD

Shut up, you!

BEN

Sorry! Sorry!

(he lowers his voice)
Now take my case. I've been here five years, and
every night they take me down for ten minutes,
then they hang me up again . . . which I regard as
very fair . . . in view of what I done . . . and if
nothing else, it's taught me to respect the
Romans, and it's taught me that you'll never get
anywhere in life unless you're prepared to do a
fair day's work for a fair day's pay . . .

BRIAN

Oh . . . Shut up!!

At that moment a CENTURION *and* TWO GUARDS *enter.*

CENTURION

Pilate wants to see you.

BRIAN

Me?

CENTURION

Come on.

BRIAN *struggles to his feet.*

BRIAN

Pilate? What does he want to see me for?

CENTURION

I think he wants to know which way up you want
to be crucified.

He laughs. The TWO SOLDIERS *smirk,* BEN *laughs up-roariously.*

BEN

. . . Nice one, centurion. Like it, like it.

CENTURION

(to Ben)
Shut up!

BRIAN *is hustled out. The door slams.*

BEN

Terrific race the Romans . . . terrific.

BRIAN *is hauled into* PILATE'S AUDIENCE CHAMBER. *It
is big and impressive, although a certain amount of
redecorating is underway. The* CENTURION *salutes.*

CENTURION

Hail Caesar.

PILATE

Hail Caesar.

CENTURION

Only one survivor, sir.

PILATE

Thwow him to the floor.

CENTURION

What sir?

PILATE
Thwow him to the floor.

CENTURION
Ah!

He indicates to the TWO ROMAN GUARDS *who throw* BRIAN *to the ground.*

PILATE
Now, what is your name, Jew?

BRIAN
Brian.

PILATE
Bwian, eh?

BRIAN
(trying to be helpful)
No, Brian.

The CENTURION *cuffs him.*

PILATE

The little wascal has spiwit.

CENTURION

Has what, sir?

PILATE

Spiwit.

CENTURION

Yes, he did, sir.

PILATE

No, no, spiwit . . . bwavado . . . a touch of dewwing-do.

CENTURION

(still not really understanding)
Ah. About eleven, sir.

PILATE

(to Brian)
So you dare to waid us.

BRIAN

(rising to his feet)
To what?

PILATE

Stwike him, centurion, vewwy woughly.

CENTURION

And throw him to the floor, sir?

PILATE

What?

CENTURION

Thwow him to the floor again, sir?

PILATE

Oh yes. Thwow him to the floor.

The CENTURION *knocks* BRIAN *hard on the side of the head again and the* TWO GUARDS *throw him to the floor.*

PILATE

Now, Jewish wapscallion.

BRIAN

I'm not Jewish . . . I'm a Roman!

PILATE

Woman?

BRIAN

No, Roman.

But he's quick enough to avoid another blow from the CENTURION.

PILATE

So, your father was a Woman. Who was he?

BRIAN

(proudly)

He was a centurion in the Jerusalem Garrison.

PILATE

Oh. What was his name?

BRIAN

Nortius Maximus.

An involuntary titter from the CENTURION.

PILATE

Centuwion, do we have anyone of that name in the gawwison?

CENTURION

Well . . . no sir.

PILATE

You sound vewwy sure . . . have you checked?

CENTURION

Well . . . no sir . . . I think it's a joke, sir . . .

like . . . Sillius Soddus . . . or . . . Biggus Dickus.

PILATE

What's so funny about Biggus Dickus?

CENTURION

Well . . . it's a . . . joke name, sir.

PILATE

I have a vewwy gweat fwend in Wome called Biggus Dickus.

Involuntary laughter from a nearby GUARD. PILATE *strides over to him.*

PILATE

Silence! What is all this insolence? You will find yourself in gladiator school vewwy quickly with wotten behaviour like that.

The GUARD *tries to stop giggling.* PILATE *turns away from him. He is very angry.*

BRIAN

　　Can I go now sir . . .

CENTURION *strikes him.*

PILATE

　　Wait till Biggus hears of this!

The GUARD *immediately breaks up again.* PILATE *turns on him.*

PILATE

　　Wight! Centuwion . . . Take him away.

CENTURION

　　Oh sir, he only . . .

I want him fighting wabid wild animals within a
week.

Yes, sir.

He starts to drag out the wretched GUARD. BRIAN
notices that little attention is being paid to him.

PILATE

I will <u>not</u> have my fwends widiculed by the
common soldiewy.

He walks slowly towards the other GUARDS.

PILATE

Now . . . anyone else feel like a little giggle
when I mention my fwend . . .
(he goes right up to one of the Guards)
Biggus . . . Dickus. He has a wife you know.
(Guards tense up)
Called Incontinentia.
(Guards relax)
Incontinentia Buttocks!
(Guards fall about laughing)

BRIAN *takes advantage of the chaos to slip away.*

PILATE

Silence! I've had enough of this wowdy wabble
webel behaviour. Stop it. Call yourselves
Pwaetowian guards. Silence!

But the GUARDS *are all hysterical by now.* PILATE
notices BRIAN *escaping.*

PILATE

Yow cwowd of cwacking-up cweeps. Seize him!
Blow your noses and seize him! Oh my bum.

The GUARDS *chase after* BRIAN *who has by now*

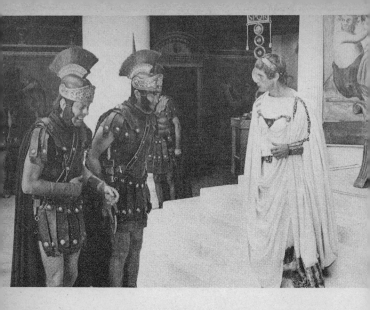

reached the doorway to a round tower. He races up the
spiral staircase just ahead of the pursuing ROMANS.
Half way up the tower he passes a WORKMAN on the
way down, who does a double take as BRIAN runs past,
and tries to warn him. Too late, the ROMANS are in hot
pursuit. Suddenly BRIAN emerges at the top of the
tower, which is only half finished, and finds the stairs
end in space. Below him is certain death, behind him
the pursuing ROMANS. He has no chance—his momen-
tum carries him off the unfinished staircase into space.

Just at that moment a passing spaceship careers underneath him, and by pure chance BRIAN lands in the
cockpit of the alien spacecraft between two STRANGE
BEINGS. They have no time to do anything about him,
they are instantly pursued by what is clearly an enemy
spaceship firing at them. The craft dodges and weaves

72

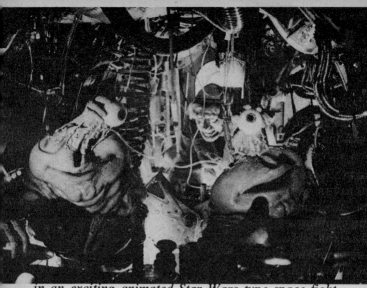

*in an exciting animated Star Wars type space fight,
climbing and weaving, and destroying the enemy craft,
before eventually being hit and plunging back to Earth
at the foot of the tower from where* BRIAN *jumped. The
craft thuds into the ground. Billowing smoke
everywhere.* BRIAN *staggers out from the wreckage.* A
PASSER-BY *looks at him with amazement, having wit-
nessed both his fall and his rescue.*

PASSER-BY
You jammy bastard!

At that moment the GUARDS *are seen still in pursuit and*
BRIAN *runs off towards the crowded market square.*

Inside the soukh there are hundreds of stalls with
STALL-HOLDERS *haggling, trading, taking coffee and
so on. At one end of the market there is a speakers'
corner, with many strangely bearded and oddly
dressed* PROPHETS *attempting to attract an audience.*

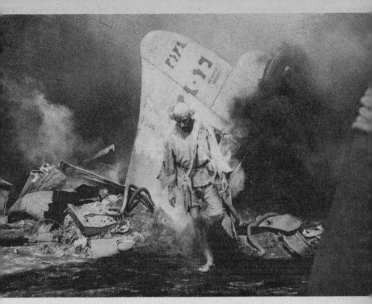

The noisiest or the most controversial are clearly doing best at attracting PASSERS-BY. A STRANGE FIGURE *with a rasta hairstyle, covered in mud, and with two severed hands on a pole waves wildly at the audience.*

BLOOD & THUNDER PROPHET
. . . and shall ride forth on a serpent's back, and the eyes shall be red with the blood of living creatures, and the whore of Babylon shall rise over the hill of excitement and throughout the land there will be a great rubbing of parts . . .

Beside him, another PROPHET *with red hair, none the less fierce, is trying to attract some of the* BLOOD & THUNDER PROPHET'S *audience.*

FALSE PROPHET
And he shall bear a nine-bladed sword. Nine bladed. Not two. Or five or seven, but nine,

which he shall wield on all wretched sinners and that includes you sir, and the horns shall be on the head . . .

In front of each PROPHET *is a* ROMAN GUARD, *clearly bored but there to break up any trouble.*

BRIAN *races into the market place. A cohort of* ROMANS *are searching the square roughly turning over baskets and shaking down* PASSERS-BY. BRIAN *appears near a rather dull little* PROPHET, *who is standing underneath the high window that backs out of* MATTHIAS' HOUSE, *the* REVOLUTIONARY HEADQUARTERS.

BORING PROPHET
And there shall in that time be rumours of things going astray, and there will be a great confusion as to where things really are, and nobody will really know where lieth those little things with the

sort of raffia work base, that has an attachment, they will not be there.

Across the square the ROMANS *appear, searching.* BRIAN *spots* HARRY THE BEARD SALESMAN *and moves towards his stall, an idea forming in his mind.*

The BORING PROPHET *drones on and on.*

BORING PROPHET
At this time a friend shall lose his friend's hammer and the young shall not know where lieth the things possessed by their fathers that their fathers put there only just the night before . . .

BRIAN *runs up to* HARRY *the beard seller's stall and grabs an artificial beard.*

BRIAN
How much? Quick!

HARRY

What?

BRIAN

It's for the wife.

HARRY

Oh. Twenty shekels.

BRIAN

Right.

HARRY

What? ´

BRIAN

There you are.
(he puts down 20 shekels)

HARRY

Wait a moment.

BRIAN

What?

HARRY

We're supposed to haggle.

BRIAN

No, no, I've got to . . .

HARRY

What do you mean no?

BRIAN

I haven't time, I've got to get . . .

HARRY

Give it back then.

BRIAN

No, no, I paid you.

HARRY

Burt!

BURT *appears, he is very big.*

BURT

Yeah!

HARRY

This bloke won't haggle.

BURT

(*looking around*)
Where are the guards?

BRIAN

Oh, alright . . . I mean do we have to . . .

HARRY

Now I want twenty for that . . .

BRIAN

I gave you twenty.

HARRY

Now are you telling me that's not worth twenty
shekels?

BRIAN

No.

HARRY

Feel the quality, that's none of yer goat.

BRIAN

Oh . . . I'll give you nineteen then.

HARRY

No, no. Do it properly.

BRIAN

What?

HARRY

Haggle properly. This isn't worth nineteen.

BRIAN

You just said it was worth twenty.

HARRY

Burt!!

BRIAN

I'll give you ten.

HARRY

That's more like it.
(*outraged*)
Ten! Are you trying to insult me? Me. With a poor
dying grandmother . . . Ten!!!?

BRIAN

Eleven.

HARRY

Now you're getting it. Eleven!!! Did I hear you
right? Eleven. This cost me twelve. You want to
ruin me.

BRIAN

Seventeen.

Seventeen!

BRIAN

Eighteen?

HARRY

No, no, no. You go to fourteen now.

BRIAN

Fourteen.

HARRY

Fourteen, are you joking?

BRIAN

That's what you told me to say.

HARRY *registers total despair.*

Tell me what to say <u>please.</u>

HARRY

Offer me fourteen.

BRIAN

I'll give you fourteen.

HARRY

(to onlookers)
He's offering me fourteen for this!

BRIAN

Fifteen.

HARRY

Seventeen. My last word. I won't take a penny
less, or strike me dead.

BRIAN

Sixteen.

HARRY

Done.

He grasps BRIAN'S *hand and shakes it.*

Nice to do business with you. Tell you what, I'll
throw in this as well.

He gives BRIAN *a gourd.*

                    BRIAN
I don't want it but thanks.

                    HARRY
Burt!

                    BURT
(appearing rapidly)
Yes?

                    BRIAN
Alright! Alright!! Thank you.

                    HARRY
Where's the sixteen then?

BRIAN

I already gave you twenty.

HARRY

Oh, yes . . . that's four I owe you then.
(starts looking for change)

BRIAN

. . . It's all right, it doesn't matter.

HARRY

Hang on.

Pause as HARRY *can't find change.* BRIAN *sees a pair of prowling* ROMANS.

BRIAN

It's all right, that's four for the gourd,—that's fine!

HARRY

Four for the gourd. Four!!!!! Look at it, that's worth ten if it's worth a shekel.

BRIAN

You just gave it to me for nothing.

HARRY

Yes, but it's *worth* ten.

BRIAN

Alright, alright.

HARRY

No, no, no. It's not worth ten. You're supposed to argue. Ten for that you must be mad.

BRIAN *runs off with the gourd, and the beard firmly on his face.*

HARRY

Ah, well there's one born every minute.

BRIAN *hastens across to the other side of the square,*

passing in front of all the prophets. Each is droning on warning the world of impending doom.

BRIAN *dodges beneath them, keeping a wary eye out for the* ROMANS *and slides up a side alley to the outside of* MATTHIAS' HOUSE.

Meanwhile inside MATTHIAS' *house* FRANCIS *has returned with the bad news of the raid, and* STAN *is striking the names of the dead* REVOLUTIONARIES *from his list.*

FRANCIS

Habbakuk. Daryl called Andy. Daniel. Job. Joshua. Judges. And Brian.

STAN

(crossing his name off)
And Brian.

REG

I now propose that all seven of these ex-brothers be now entered in the minutes as probationary martyrs to the cause.

STAN

I second that, Reg.

REG

Thank you, Loretta. Siblings!! Let us not be disheartened. One total catastrophe like this is just the beginning! Their glorious deaths shall unite us all.

MATTHIAS

Look out!

The REVOLUTIONARIES *all race to hide. They hide extremely badly.* STAN *picks up a sheet,* REG *nips under the table.* BRIAN *enters with a false beard on.*

(he looks round)
Hello, hello . . . . Reg?

REG

(from under the table)
Go away!

BRIAN

Reg! It's me, Brian.

REG

Go on! Get off out of it.

BRIAN *sees* STAN *under the sheet.*

BRIAN

Stan!

STAN

Piss off.

ALL

Yeah. Clear off.

A heavy imperious knocking on the door. All heads of the REVOLUTIONARIES, *which have appeared for a moment disappear instantly.*

ALL

Oh shit!

MATTHIAS

Coming!

He starts looking round for somewhere for BRIAN *to hide. More knocking. He pushes* BRIAN *behind some curtains.* BRIAN *finds himself on a balcony high up above the city. There is immediately an ominous creak and the balcony settles. A bit of dust falls and* BRIAN *realises he is on a very unsafe perch.*

From below we hear the drone of the BORING PROPHET.

BRIAN *looks down and sees all the* PROPHETS *below him.*

Meanwhile MATTHIAS *heads towards the door.*

MATTHIAS

I'm an old man . . . my eyes are dim . . . I cannot see . . .

A squad of ROMAN SOLDIERS *outside.*

CENTURION

Are you Matthias?

MATTHIAS

Yes.

CENTURION

We have reason to believe you may be hiding one Brian of Nazareth, a member of the terrorist organisation—the People's Front of Judea.

MATTHIAS

Me? . . . No . . . I'm just a poor old man . . . I have no time for law-breakers. My sight is poor, my legs are grey, my ears are gnarled, my eyes are old and bent.

CENTURION

Quiet! Silly person. Guards! Search the house.

TWO GUARDS *go in at the double. Followed by two more. Followed by two more, followed by about twelve more in formation. They go clattering in.*

CENTURION

You know the punishment laid down by Roman law for harbouring a known criminal.

MATTHIAS

No.

CENTURION

Crucifixion.

86

MATTHIAS

Oh.

CENTURION

Nasty eh?

MATTHIAS

Could be worse.

CENTURION

"Could be worse"? What d'you mean?

MATTHIAS

Well you could be stabbed.

CENTURION

Stabbed? That takes a second. Crucifixion lasts hours. It's a slow, horrible death.

MATTHIAS

Well at least it gets you out in the open air.

CENTURION

You're weird.

The ROMAN SOLDIERS *come clanking out of the house.*

SERGEANT

No sir, couldn't find anything, sir.

CENTURION

Alright . . . but don't worry—you've not seen the last of us—weirdo!

MATTHIAS

Big nose!

CENTURION

Watch it!

The ROMAN GUARDS *march off.* MATTHIAS *shuts the door thankfully.*

MATTHIAS

Phew that was lucky.

The hiders emerge.

BRIAN

I'm sorry, Reg.

REG

Oh it's all right siblings, he's sorry. He's sorry he led the Fifth Legion straight to our official headquarters. Well, that's all right. Sit down. Have a scone. Make yourself at home. You CUNT!! You stupid, bird-brained, flat-headed . . .

There is another burst of loud knocking. At once the REVOLUTIONARIES *go into hiding. Reluctantly* BRIAN *backs out on to the balcony. A crack appears and* BRIAN *hangs on desperately to support his own weight.*

MATTHIAS

My legs are old and bent, my ears are grizzled.

He opens the door. The ROMANS *are outside again.* Yes?

CENTURION

There's one place we didn't look. Guards.

CENTURION *nods his head and the* ROMAN SOLDIERS *pour in again.*

MATTHIAS

Have pity. I'm just a poor old man. My sight is weak, my eyes are poor and my nose is knackered.

CENTURION

Have you ever <u>seen</u> anyone crucified?

MATTHIAS

Crucifixion's a doddle.

CENTURION

(hurt)
Don't keep saying that.

The SOLDIERS *come rushing out.*

We found this spoon, sir.

CENTURION

Alright Sergeant.
(to Matthias)
We'll be back. Oddball!

MATTHIAS *shuts the door and turns to the others with a sigh of relief. As they all start to emerge there is yet another knock on the door. They hide again as* BRIAN *scuttles back on to the balcony. This time the whole balcony shudders.* BRIAN *clings tighter to it.*

Outside they can hear the CENTURION *shouting.*

CENTURION

Open up!

MATTHIAS

(indignantly)
You haven't given us time to hide!

Suddenly BRIAN'S *balcony collapses and* BRIAN *plummets down towards the head of the* BORING PROPHET, *knocking the* BORING PROPHET *cleanly off his perch, straight into a basket. There is a smattering of applause from the crowd. They clearly like tricks. Even the* BLOOD AND THUNDER PROPHETS *pause for a moment—then redouble their efforts.*

BRIAN *looks down and sees a* ROMAN SOLDIER *standing directly at his feet, looking up at him inquiringly.* BRIAN *looks to left and right at the other* PROPHETS *and then back at the* SOLDIER *before he realises what is expected of him. He takes a deep breath and begins.*

BRIAN

Don't pass judgement on other people, or you might get judged yourself.

The ROMAN SOLDIER *looks back, satisfied that* BRIAN
is a bonafide false prophet.

Passer-by COLIN *stops.*

COLIN

What?

BRIAN

I said 'Don't pass judgement on other people or
else you might get judged too'.

COLIN

Who, me?

BRIAN

Yes.

COLIN

Oh right. Thank you.

COLIN *goes off happily with his advice.*

BRIAN

Well . . . not just you, all of you.

A man, DENNIS, *has been staring at* BRIAN'S *gourd.*
EDDIE, ELSIE, FRANK *and* GEOFFREY *are wandering by.*

DENNIS

That's a nice gourd.

BRIAN

What?

DENNIS

How much do you want for the gourd?

BRIAN

I don't . . . you can have it.

DENNIS

Have it?

BRIAN *gives it to him.*

BRIAN

Yes. Consider the lilies . . .

90

DENNIS

Don't you want to haggle?

BRIAN

No. In the fields.

DENNIS

What's wrong with it then?

BRIAN

Nothing, take it.

GEOFFREY

(puzzled)
Consider the lilies?

BRIAN

Well, the birds then.

EDDIE

What birds?

91

BRIAN

Any birds.

EDDIE

Why?

BRIAN

Well . . . have <u>they</u> got jobs?

ARTHUR

Who?

BRIAN

The birds.

EDDIE

Have the birds got jobs?

FRANK

What's the matter with him?

ARTHUR

He says the birds are scrounging.

BRIAN

No, look, the point is they're doing alright, aren't they?

FRANK

And good luck to 'em.

EDDIE

They're very pretty.

BRIAN

Right! Right! They eat but they don't grow anything do they?

FRANK

Well, nobody's asking 'em to.

BRIAN

O.K. And you're more important than they are, right? Well, there you are then. What are you <u>worrying</u> about. There you are. See?

EDDIE

I'm worrying about what you got against birds.

BRIAN

I haven't got anything against birds. Consider the lilies . . .

ARTHUR

He's having a go at the flowers now.

EDDIE

Oh, give the little flowers a chance.

DENNIS

I'll give you one for it.

BRIAN

It's yours.

DENNIS

Two then.

BRIAN

Look, there was this man and he had two servants . . .

ARTHUR

What were their names?

BRIAN

What?

ARTHUR

What were they called?

BRIAN

I don't know. And he gave them some talents.

ELSIE

You don't know.

BRIAN

Well, it doesn't matter.

ARTHUR

He doesn't know what they were called.

BRIAN

They were called Simon and Adrian. Now . . .

ARTHUR

Oh! You said you didn't know.

BRIAN

It really doesn't matter.
The point is there were these two servants . . .

SAM

He's making it up as he goes along.

BRIAN

No I'm not . . . or wait a moment, were there
three?

EDDIE

Oh he's terrible isn't he?

ARTHUR

Terrible.

BRIAN

Three . . . well <u>stewards</u> really . . .

General eye raising to heaven.

ARTHUR

Tch tch tch.

A squad of ROMANS *who have been observing all this
start to stride purposefully towards* BRIAN.

BRIAN *sees them and panics.*

BRIAN

(desperately, to his dwindling audience)
Er, hear this! Er . . . Blessed are they . . . who
convert their neighbour's ox . . . for they shall
inhibit their girth . . . and to them only shall be
given . . .

The ROMANS *walk past him at this point and he realises
that they were merely rejoining their platoon. The*

ROMAN *who was standing beneath him has also gone with them.*

BRIAN *watches the* ROMANS *go.*

BRIAN

. . . and to them only shall . . . be . . .
given . . .

His voice trails off as he watches the ROMANS *leaving the square. His audience is waiting for him to finish his sentence.*

BRIAN *breathes in relief and relaxes leaning back against the wall.*

ELSIE

What?

BRIAN

Hmmm?

ELSIE

Shall be given what?

BRIAN

Oh, nothing.

BRIAN *climbs down from the ledge to leave. But the crowd won't leave him now.*

ARTHUR

Hey! What were you going to say?

BRIAN

Nothing.

ARTHUR

Yes you were.

ELSIE

You were going to say something.

BRIAN

No I wasn't.

ARTHUR

Tell us before you go.

BRIAN

I wasn't going to say anything. I'd finished.

ELSIE

No you hadn't.

A YOUTH *arrives.*

YOUTH

What won't he tell us?

ELSIE

I don't know.

YOUTH

Is it a secret?

BRIAN

No . . .

YOUTH

Is it?

ELSIE

It must be. Otherwise he'd tell us.

ARTHUR

(to Brian)
What is the secret?

BRIAN

Leave me alone.

OTHERS

Yes! Tell us the secret!

More people join the crowd pressing forward after
BRIAN *as he makes his way through the market.*

YOUTH

What is this secret?

GIRL

Is it the secret of Eternal Life?

ELSIE

He won't say.

ARTHUR

Of course not—if I knew the secret of Eternal Life, I wouldn't say.

BRIAN *is thrusting his way through the now rapidly growing throng. A hard core is keeping up with him and pestering him.*

BRIAN

Leave me alone.

BRIAN *looks around desperately to make sure there are no* ROMANS.

GIRL

Just tell us, <u>please</u>!

97

Tell <u>us</u>! We were here first.

ELSIE
(turning to the gathering crowd)
Go away the rest of you.

REST OF CROWD
No! What's going on?

More join the crowd.

YOUTH
We were here first.

ARTHUR
No you weren't, we were.

GIRL
Tell us, Master.

BRIAN *dives through the crowd, which is becoming increasingly excited, and bumps into* DENNIS, *who is still holding the gourd.*

DENNIS
My final offer. Five!

BRIAN
Go away.

The GIRL *approaches* DENNIS.

GIRL
Is that . . . <u>his</u> gourd?

DENNIS
It's under offer.

GIRL
(taking the gourd and raising it aloft)
This is his gourd!

DENNIS
Ten then.

GIRL

It is <u>His</u> gourd! We will carry it for you
Master . . .

The crowd looks up. BRIAN *has disappeared.*

YOUTH

He's gone! He's been taken up!

ALL

He's been taken up!

ARTHUR

No, there he is!

Indicates BRIAN *disappearing round a corner. At once
the crowd gives chase.*

CROWD

Master! Master!

99

BRIAN *appears at the gates of the city, accelerating fast. Behind him the rumble of a pursuing crowd.* BRIAN *looks back desperately and runs up a path which takes him along the lower slopes of the hill towards Calvary. As he runs, he slips and one of his sandals comes off. He is about to retrieve it, when he sees his followers pouring out of the City gates. They see him and immediately give chase.* BRIAN *turns and runs off. The crowd approaches the sandal.*

ELSIE

(holds up Brian's shoe)
Look!

GIRL

Follow the Gourd! The Holy Gourd of Jerusalem.

YOUTH

Get off!

EDDIE

Come on! Follow the Shoe!

YOUTH

Bring the sandal.

GEORGE

No it's a shoe!

HARRY

Put it on!

GEORGE

Clear off!

EDDIE

I will keep the shoe and put other shoes with it.

HARRY

It's a sandal.

EDDIE

No it isn't.

ARTHUR
Follow the shoe-ites!

YOUTH
Follow the way of the sandalites.

ARTHUR
But cast away our own shoes . . .

Some do.

ARTHUR
He has given us a sign.

EDDIE
He has given us a shoe.

ARTHUR
The shoe is the sign. Let us follow his example.

YOUTH

What d'you mean?

ARTHUR

Let us, like him, <u>carry</u> one shoe . . . and let the other be upon our feet. For this is his sign, that all who follow him shall do likewise.

GIRL

Cast off the shoes! Follow the gourd.

EDDIE

No! Gather shoes! . . . We must gather shoes together in abundance.
(*turns to man next to him*)
Let me . . .

He starts trying to get the man's shoe off.

GEORGE

Get off!

YOUTH

No! It is a sign that we must, like him, think not of the things of the body but of the face and head.

He kneels in prayer. Immediately someone tries to take his shoe.

YOUTH

Ouch.

EDDIE

Give me your shoe.

GIRL

Come! All ye who call yourself Gourdenes!

HARRY

Keep the shoe.

SPIKE

Let us pray.

But SPIKE *is left alone as the crowd sets off in pursuit of* BRIAN, *who is by now racing, or rather limping along a steep upland path. He looks behind him, takes a deep breath and scrambles up between hanging rocks. He climbs and climbs higher and higher, still pursued by about a hundred raving* FOLLOWERS. *At the hill top* BRIAN *pauses and looks down to see the* FOLLOWERS *still coming up the path from below. He can turn neither left nor right. To one side there is a hole, no more than six feet across but quite deep, in which crouches a bearded mystic, in a meditative position. This is* BRIAN'S *chance.*

BRIAN

Hey!

SIMON *the Holy Man looks up.*

BRIAN

Is there another way down?

SIMON'S *face takes on a look of horror. Eyes popping and lips pressed tight together he shakes his head.*

SIMON

Mmmm Mmmm.

BRIAN

Is there another <u>path</u> down to the river?

SIMON

(deliberately saying nothing and motioning to
BRIAN *to go away)*
Mmmmmm.

BRIAN

(hearing his FOLLOWERS)
Please help me! I've got to get away.

SIMON

Mmm Mmmm Mmmmm.

The FOLLOWERS *are getting desperately close. Without*

waiting for them to see him, BRIAN *leaps into the hole.*
He lands on top of the bearded HOLY MAN *who*
screams.

SIMON

Ow! MY FOOT!!!

He grabs his foot in agony, but suddenly a fresh agony
wracks him.

SIMON

Oh damn! Damn, damn, damn!

BRIAN

(desperately)
Ssh! I'm sorry.

SIMON

Oh . . . Damn . . . damn and blast and damn
. . . ohhhh!!!

BRIAN

Sssh! Sssh! I'm sorry!

SIMON

Don't "ssh" me! Eighteen years of total silence
and you ssh <u>me!!</u>

BRIAN

What?

SIMON

I've kept my vows for eighteen years.
Not a recognisable articulate sound . . .

BRIAN

I'm sorry . . . I didn't realise.

SIMON

Not a word. And then you come along.

BRIAN

Please be quiet . . . just for another five
minutes . . .

105

Oh there's no point in being quiet, now. I might as
well enjoy myself. The times in the last eighteen
years when I've wanted to shout and sing! De da
dum. And shout my name out. Oh I'm alive! Hava
Nagila.

BRIAN *slaps his hand over his mouth, but the* HERMIT
fights back with scrawny strength.

SIMON

Please!

SIMON

De Da Dum.
*(he goes into rough tuneless singing, but very
loudly)*
Hava Nagila!! Hava . . .

BRIAN *desperately slaps a hand over his mouth.*

SIMON

I'm alive! I'm alive!!!

Cut to the reactions of the FOLLOWERS *who react to the
sound, marvelling.*

BRIAN *fights and struggles rather gracelessly with the
yelling shouting noisy old* HERMIT.

SIMON

Hello Trees! Hello Sky! Hello rocks!!
Oh it's a lovely day today. Hava Nagila! . . .

We see BRIAN *rear up briefly out of the hole holding the*
HERMIT'S *mouth, but he reacts in horror to the approach of his* FOLLOWERS *and ducks down but the
hermit breaks loose again. The* HERMIT'S *voice suddenly tails off as he sees what* BRIAN *has seen.*

SIMON *stops. His eyes boggle. The* FOLLOWERS *approach the hole. They fall to the ground.*

CROWD

The Master! We have found him! A miracle! His
shoe was right! Blessed be the shoe! The sandal!
The gourd! The Miracle of the Shoe etc. etc.

ARTHUR

Speak to us . . . Speak to us . . .

CROWD

Speak to us . . .

BRIAN

Go away!

CROWD

A blessing! A blessing!!

ARTHUR

How shall we go away Master?

BRIAN

Just go away . . . leave me alone.

ELSIE

Give us a sign.

ARTHUR

He <u>has</u> shown us a sign. He has brought us here to his place.

BRIAN

I did not bring you here. You just followed me.

EDDIE

It's still a good sign, by any standard.

ARTHUR

Master! Your people have walked many miles to be with you. They are weary and have not eaten.

BRIAN

Look it's not my fault they haven't eaten.

ARTHUR

There is no food in this high mountain.

BRIAN

What about the juniper bushes over there.

CROWD

A miracle! A miracle!

ELSIE

The bushes have been made fruitful by his word.

YOUTH

They have brought forth juniper berries.

BRIAN

Of course they've brought forth juniper berries . . . they're juniper bushes! What d'you expect?

YOUTH

Show us another miracle!

ARTHUR

Do not tempt him, shallow ones. Is not the
miracle of the juniper bushes enough?

SIMON *sees the crowd pulling the juniper bushes to
pieces.*

SIMON

I say! Those are <u>my</u> juniper bushes!

ARTHUR

They are a gift from God.

SIMON

They're all I've bloody got to eat! 'Ere 'ere, get
away from those bushes!

A MAN *falls in front of* BRIAN.

HARRY

Lord! I am affected by a bald patch!

A BLIND MAN *with a white stick pushes his way to the
front of the crowd.*

BLIND MAN

I'm healed! The master has healed me!

BRIAN

I never touched him!

BLIND MAN

I was blind and now I can see.
*(he throws his white stick away and stumbles
instantly into the hole)*
Aargh!

SIMON *runs up to* BRIAN.

SIMON

Tell them to stop it!
(to crowd)

I hadn't said a word for eighteen years till he came along.

ALL

A miracle! He <u>is</u> the Messiah.

SIMON

He <u>hurt</u> my foot!!

ALL

(*offering their feet*)
Hurt my foot Lord!! Hurt my foot. Please!

ARTHUR

Hail Messiah!

BRIAN

I'm <u>not</u> the Messiah.

ARTHUR

I say you are Lord, and I should know, I've followed a few.

Hail Messiah.

SIMON *runs over to the juniper berry pickers trying to stop them.*

SIMON

Stop it! Stop it!

BRIAN

I am not the Messiah, will you please listen! I am <u>not</u> the Messiah. D'you understand. <u>Honestly</u>!

GIRL

Only the true Messiah denies his divinity.

BRIAN

What!? Oh!
(in exasperation)
What sort of a chance does <u>that</u> give me?
. . . Alright! I <u>am</u> the Messiah!

Uproar.

CROWD

He is! He is the Messiah!

They all fall and worship him.

BRIAN

Now fuck off!!!

Long pause.

ARTHUR

How shall we fuck off O Lord?

BRIAN

Just . . . go away. Leave me alone.

SIMON *comes back.*

SIMON

(accusingly to BRIAN.*)*

You told these people to eat my juniper berries.

BRIAN

Look . . . I only . . .

SIMON

You break my bloody foot, you break my vow of
silence, and now you try and clean up on my
juniper bushes.

SIMON *begins attacking* BRIAN. ARTHUR *at once rushes
in to intervene.*

ARTHUR

This is the Messiah—the chosen one.

SIMON

No he's not! He's just . . .

ARTHUR

An unbeliever!!

ALL

An unbeliever!!

ARTHUR

Persecute! Death to the unbelievers!

BRIAN

Look. No. He only . . .

The crowd manhandle SIMON *away lifting him up and above them.* SIMON *struggles desperately as* BRIAN *tries hopelessly to intervene.*

ALL

A heretic! Kill! Persecute . . . Persecute the heretic!

BRIAN

Leave him alone . . . please . . !

But BRIAN *is powerless to prevent the mob violence that has broken out, and he can only watch helplessly as the crowd carry away the nearly naked* SIMON *to his doom. He suddenly realises that he is at last alone, and is about to slip away when he sees* JUDITH *standing in front of him, looking at him with admiration. An idea occurs to* BRIAN.

Dawn over a large cut-out of Jerusalem. Usual dawn clichés. Cocks crowing, birds twittering, sound effects men working overtime.

BRIAN *stirs in his bed, and opens his eyes, to see the naked sleeping form of* JUDITH *beside him. Clearly certain unspecified but apparently rude behaviour has taken place during the night.* BRIAN *smiles warmly at the memory, gets out of bed, yawns and wanders over to the window. He throws open the shutters and flings his arms back to stretch. He is quite naked. Suddenly he freezes in mid-stretch, horrified. A vast crowd thronging the courtyard outside his bedroom window is looking up at him.*

113

CROWD

Look! There he is. The chosen one has woken!

There are at least four hundred people outside. BRIAN *slams the shutters and retreats in panic from the window. From downstairs he hears his* MOTHER'S *voice.*

MANDY

(off)
Brian! Brian!

As he struggles into his robe, the door of his room flies open and MANDY *storms in.*

BRIAN

Oh, hello Mother.

MANDY

Don't you 'hello Mother' me! What are all those people doing out there?

BRIAN

Oh, er, well . . !

MANDY

Come on, what have you been up to, my lad?

BRIAN

I think they must have popped by for something.

MANDY

"Popped by!" "Swarmed by" more like!
There's a multitude out there!

BRIAN

They started following me yesterday.

MANDY

Well, they can stop following you right now!

BRIAN *hesitates*. MANDY *goes to the window and opens the shutters.*

MANDY

(to the crowd)
Now stop following my son. You ought to be ashamed of yourselves.

CROWD

The Messiah. The Messiah. Show us the Messiah.

MANDY

The <u>who?</u>

CROWD

The Messiah.

MANDY

There's no Messiah in here. There's a mess all right, but no Messiah. Now go away.

CROWD

Brian! Brian!

MANDY

Right my lad, what have you been up to?

BRIAN

Well, mother . . .

MANDY

Out with it! Come on!

BRIAN

They think I'm the Messiah, mother.

MANDY *clips him across the ear.*

MANDY

What have you been telling them?

BRIAN

Nothing.

MANDY

You're only making it worse for yourself.

She clips him again and then turns as JUDITH *appears*

116

from BRIAN'S *bed stark naked.* MANDY *stares speech-lessly as* JUDITH *comes forward and stands between* BRIAN *and his mother protectively.*

JUDITH
Let me explain Mrs. Cohen! Your son is a born leader. These people out there are following him because he will lead them with hope to a new world, a better future.

MANDY
(eventually, to BRIAN*)*
<u>WHO</u>'s that???!!

BRIAN
(terrified)
It's Judith, mum. Judith . . . mother . . . mother . . . Judith

MANDY *moves forward to thump him again, but is distracted by the growing shouts of the crowd for* BRIAN. *She returns to the window.*

> CROWD
>
> Show us the Messiah.
>
> MANDY
>
> Now you listen. He's not the Messiah, he's a very naughty boy. Now go away.
>
> CROWD
>
> Who are you?
>
> MANDY
>
> I'm his mother that's who.
>
> CROWD
>
> Behold his Mother. Behind his Mother!! Hail to

thee, mother of Brian. All hail. Blessed art thou.
Hosanna. All praise to thee, now and always!!!!

MANDY

Now don't think you can get round me that way.
He's not coming out and that's my final word.
Now shove off!

CROWD

No!

MANDY

Did you hear what I said?

CROWD

Yes!!

MANDY

Oh, I see. It's like that is it?

CROWD

Yes.

MANDY

Alright, you can see him for <u>one</u> minute, but not
one second more, do you understand?

CROWD

(*reluctantly*)
Yes.

MANDY

Promise?

CROWD

Well . . . alright.

MANDY

Right. Here he is then. Come on, Brian. Come
and talk to them.

BRIAN

But mum, Judith.

MANDY

Leave that Welsh tart alone.

BRIAN

I don't really want to, Mum.

BRIAN *moves forward. The crowd cheers, "Hosanna," "The Master," "All Hail" etc. The pandemonium dies down.*

BRIAN

Good morning.

CROWD

A blessing! A blessing!

More pandemonium.

BRIAN

No, please. Please. Please listen.
(they quieten)

I've got one or two things to say.

CROWD

Tell us. Tell us both of them!!

BRIAN

Look . . . you've got it all wrong. You don't
need to follow me. You don't need to follow
anybody. You've got to think for yourselves.
You're all individuals.

CROWD

Yes, we're all individuals.

BRIAN

You're all different.

CROWD

Yes, we _are_ all different.

DENNIS

I'm not.

CROWD

Sssshhh!

BRIAN

Well, that's it. You've all got to work it out for
yourselves.

CROWD

Yes, yes!! We've got to work it out for ourselves.

BRIAN

Exactly.

CROWD

Tell us more.

BRIAN

No, no, that's the point. Don't let anyone tell you
what to do. Otherwise . . . Ow!

MANDY _drags him away by his ear._

MANDY

That's enough.

She propels him out of sight.

                    CROWD
(disappointed)
Ooooh. That wasn't a minute!

                    MANDY
Oh yes it was.

                    CROWD
Oh no it wasn't!

                    MANDY
Now stop that, and go away.

                    YOUTH
Excuse me.

                    MANDY
Yes?

YOUTH

Are you a virgin?

MANDY

I beg your pardon.

YOUTH

Well, if it's not a personal question, are you a virgin?

MANDY

If it's not a personal question. How much more personal can you get? Now piss off.

YOUTH

She is.

EVERYONE

Yeah. Definitely.

BRIAN *opens the door leading downstairs. And then gawks. Below him in* MANDY'S *kitchen there is a scene of great activity. The* REVOLUTIONARIES *are everywhere, carrying in a table, controlling queues, organizing everyone. A lot of the lay public are also in the room in various groups, milling about.* REG *is manically active.*

REG

Line up along there please. Get 'em in two rows Stan. Those with gifts, come forward. Incurables, I'm afraid you'll just have to wait for a few minutes.

MAN

Will he endorse fish?

REG

You'll have to see Sibling Francis about endorsements. And keep the noise down a bit <u>please</u>!! Those possessed by devils, try to keep them under control a bit, can't you.

REG *looks up and sees* BRIAN.

REG

Morning, Saviour.

The crowd surges toward BRIAN *and the* REV-
OLUTIONARIES *go to help him.*

FRANCIS

Come on, give him space, don't push, mind your
backs.

BRIAN *is in no mood for this and he walks through the
crowd without slowing his pace.*

MAN

My little boy just loved your juniper berries
miracle.

WOMAN

(rudely)
Lay your hand here quick.

FRANCIS

Don't jostle the Chosen One. Please!

REG

Don't push that baby in the Saviour's face.

MR. GREGORY

I say, I say, could he just see my wife? She has a
headache.

REG

She'll have to wait I'm afraid.

GREGORY

It's very bad and we have a lunch appointment.

REG

Look, the lepers are queuing . . .

FRANCIS

Don't push!

Brian, can I introduce you to Mr. Papadopoulos
who's letting us have the Mount on Saturday.

But BRIAN *slips out through the back door and descends some steps into* MANDY'S *garden where he sits,
head in hands.*

Suddenly a voice assails him.

> OTTO

Hail leader.

> BRIAN

What?

> OTTO

Oh. I'm so sorry. Have you seen the new leader?

> BRIAN

The what?

> OTTO

The new leader. Where is the new leader? I wish
to hail him. Hail leader. See.

> BRIAN

Oh. Who are you?

> OTTO

My name. Is. Otto.

> BRIAN

Oh.

> OTTO

Yes. Otto. It's time, you know . . .

> BRIAN

What?

> OTTO

. . . Time that we Jews racially purified
ourselves.

BRIAN

Oh.

OTTO

He's right, you know. The new leader. We need more living room. We must move into the traditionally Jewish areas of Samaria.

BRIAN

What about the Samaritans?

OTTO

Well, we can put them in little camps. And after Samaria we must move into Jordan and create a great Jewish state that will last a thousand years.

BRIAN

Yes, I'm not sure that I . . .

OTTO

Oh, I grow so impatient you know. To see the Leader that has been promised our people for centuries. The Leader who will save Israel by ridding it of the scum of non-Jewish people, making it pure, no foreigners, no gypsies, no riff-raff.

BRIAN

Shhh. Otto.

OTTO

What, the Leader? Hail Leader!

BRIAN

No no. It's dangerous.

OTTO

Oh, danger: There is no danger.
(flicks his fingers)
Men!

A Phalanx of armed, rather sinister, men appear from the shadows and fall in.

OTTO

Impressive, eh?

BRIAN

Yes.

OTTO

Yes, we are a thoroughly trained suicide squad.

BRIAN

Ah-hah.

OTTO

Oh yes, we can commit suicide within twenty seconds.

BRIAN

Twenty seconds?

OTTO

You don't believe me?

BRIAN

Well . . . yes . . .

OTTO

I think you question me.

BRIAN

No. No.

OTTO

I can see you do not believe me.

BRIAN

No no, I do.

OTTO

Enough. I prove it to you. Squad.

SQUAD

Hail Leader.

OTTO

Co-mmit Suicide.

They all pull out their swords with military precision

*and plunge them into themselves in time, falling in a big
heap on the ground. Dead.*

OTTO

(with pride)
See.

BRIAN

Yes.

OTTO

I think now you believe me, yes?

BRIAN

Yes.

OTTO

I think now I prove it to you, huh?

BRIAN

Yes, you certainly did.

OTTO

All dead.

BRIAN

Yes.

OTTO

Not one living.

BRIAN

No.

OTTO

You see, they are all of them quite dead. See I
kick this one. He's dead. And this one's dead, I
tread on his head. And he's dead. And he's dead.
All good Jewish boys, no foreigners. But they
died a hero's death and their names will be
remembered forever. Helmut . . . Johnny . . .
the little guy . . . er . . . the other fat one . . .
their names will be remembered . . . eventually
. . . forever. So now I go. Hail Leader.

BRIAN

Wait Otto. You can't just leave them all here.

OTTO

Why not—they're all dead.

One of the 'corpses' farts. There is a giggle.

OTTO

Wait a minute. There is somebody here who is not
dead. There is somebody here who is only
pretending to be dead. Stand up you.

*One of the bodies stands up sheepishly. As he does so,
he stands on someone else who quite clearly says 'Ow.'*

OTTO

Who said 'ow'? You're not dead either. Neither
are you. Stand up, stand up, all of you. Oh my
heck, is there not even one dead?

They have all stood up averting their eyes in shame.

HELMUT

No sir. Not one.

ADOLF

We thought it was a practice sir.

OTTO

Oh my cock. Tomorrow as punishment, you will
eat—pork sausages!

There is a horrified muttering at this suggestion. OTTO
turns sharply to BRIAN.

OTTO

O.K. Tell the Leader we are ready to die for him
the moment he gives the sign.

BRIAN

What sign?

OTTO

The sign that is the sign, that shall be the sign.
Men, forward.

OTTO'S MEN *march away singing their exciting song.*

OTTO'S MEN'S SONG
There's a man we call our leader
Who's fine and strong and brave
And we'll follow him unquestioning
Towards an early grave
He gives us hope of sacrifice
And a chance to die in vain
And if we're one of the lucky ones
We'll live to die again.

BRIAN

Silly bugger.

JUDITH *comes down the steps towards him. At the sight of her he perks up, and his mind reverts to country matters.*

JUDITH

Brian! You were fantastic!

BRIAN

Well you weren't so bad yourself.

JUDITH

No no . . . What you said just now was quite extraordinary.

BRIAN

What? Oh . . . that . . . was it?

JUDITH

We don't need leaders. You're so right. Reg has been dominating us for too long.

BRIAN

Well yes.

JUDITH

It needed saying and you said it. It's our revolution, we can all do it together. We're all behind you Brian. The revolution's in your hands now.

CENTER>BRIAN</CENTER>
No, that's not what I meant at all!

A familiar ROMAN CENTURION'S *hand claps itself down on* BRIAN'S *shoulder. A group of* ROMAN SOLDIERS *surround him, thrusting* JUDITH *brutally aside.*

CENTURION
You're fuckin' nicked, my old beauty.

JUDITH *struggles briefly with a* SOLDIER *but is thrown aside as* BRIAN *is dragged off.*

BRIAN *is kicked hard on the side of the head. He is once again in* PILATE'S *Audience Chamber.* BIGGUS *is lying on a couch.*

PILATE
Well, Brian, you've given us a good wun for our money.

BRIAN

A what?

He is thumped by the GUARD.

PILATE

This time I guawantee you will not escape.
Guard, do we have any cwucifixions today?

GUARD

A hundred and thirty-nine, Sir, special
celebration, Passover, Sir.

PILATE

Wight. Well, we now have 140. Nice wound
number, eh Biggus?

The CENTURION *strides in rather agitatedly. He gives a
perfunctory salute to* PILATE.

CENTURION

Sir! The crowd outside is getting a bit restless!
Permission to disperse them please.

PILATE

Disperse them, but I haven't addwessed them yet.

CENTURION

You're not thinking of giving it a miss this year,
sir?

PILATE

Giving it a miss Centuwion? My addwess is one
of the high spots of the Passover.

The GUARDS *exchange looks and suppress smiles.*

PILATE

Biggus Dickus has come all the way fwom Wome
especially to hear it.

BIGGUS DICKUS, *a large, over dressed, slightly effete
Roman, nods.*

133

CENTURION
It's just that the crowd is in a funny mood today, sir.

PILATE
I'm surpwised to see you wattled by a wabble of wowdy webels, centuwion.

CENTURION
A bit thundery, sir.

An uncomfortable silence. No one is quite sure where to look.

PILATE *turns to* BRIAN.

PILATE
Take him away, and cwucify him well.

The GUARD *salutes and drags* BRIAN *away.* PILATE

turns and makes for the entrance to the forum. The
CENTURION *has one last attempt at discussion.*

CENTURION
I really wouldn't if I were you, sir.

PILATE
Out of the way, Centuwion!

BIGGUS
Let me come with you Pontiuth. I may be of
thome athithtence if there ith a thudden crithith.

The CENTURION *looks to the skies—mute appeal for
help. Then turns and follows them outside.*

Meanwhile—the REVOLUTIONARIES *are back at*
MATTHIAS' *house having another meeting.*

Right, now item 4. Attainment of world
supremacy within the next four years. Sibling
Francis, you've been doing some work on this.

FRANCIS

Yeah, thank you, Reg. Well, quite frankly
siblings, I think five years is optimistic unless we
can smash the Roman Empire within the next
twelve months.

REG

Twelve months?

FRANCIS

Yes, twelve months, and let's face it, as Empires
go, this is the big one so we've got to get up off
our arses and stop just talking about it.

ALL

Hear, hear.

STAN

I agree it's action that counts, not words, and we
need action now.

ALL

Hear, hear.

REG

You're right, we could sit around here all day
passing resolutions, making clever speeches, but
it's not going to shift one Roman soldier.

FRANCIS

So let's stop gabbing on about it. It's completely
pointless and it's getting us nowhere.

ALL

Right.

STAN

I agree, this is a complete waste of time.

Agreed.

REG

Good, that's settled then.

JUDITH *rushes in*.

JUDITH

They've arrested Brian!

REG

What?

JUDITH

They've dragged him off. They're going to crucify him.

REG

Right, this calls for immediate discussion.

JUDITH

What?

STAN

New motion?

REG

Completely new motion. That, er, that there be immediate action.

FRANCIS

Once the vote has been taken.

REG

Of course, once the vote's been taken, you can't act on a resolution till the vote's been taken.

JUDITH

Reg, let's go now, please.

REG

Right. In the light of fresh information from Sibling Judith.

Not so fast, Reg.

JUDITH

Reg, for God's sake. It's perfectly simple. All you've got to do is go out of that door now and try to stop the Romans nailing him up. It's happening, Reg. Something's actually happening, Reg, can't you understand—Ohh!

She rushes out.

REG

Oh dear . . . another little ego trip from the feminists.

STAN

What!

REG

Oh, sorry Loretta. Now then, Francis, I believe you had a resolution to put before the committee?

BRIAN *is now inside the cells, manacled, in a line of* PRISONERS *shuffling forward. A rather understanding, kindly Roman officer,* NISUS WETTUS, *is checking them off on a list, as each one comes forward.*

NISUS

Next? Crucifixion?

1ST PRISONER

Yes.

NISUS

Good . . . right.

Ticks him off. JAILER *undoes the manacles.*

NISUS

Out of the door, line on the left, one cross each . . . next . . .

Another PRISONER *steps forward.*

NISUS

Crucifixion?

2ND PRISONER

Yes.

NISUS

Good . . . Out of the door, line on the left, one
cross each . . . Next?

Another PRISONER *steps forward.*

Crucifixion?

MR. CHEEKY

Er . . . no . . . freedom . . .

NISUS

What?

139

MR. CHEEKY

Er . . . freedom for me . . . They said I hadn't done anything so I could go free and live on an island somewhere.

NISUS

(looks at book)
Well, that's jolly good . . . In that case . . . *(he goes to strike out Mr. Cheeky's name)*

MR. CHEEKY

No . . . no . . . it's crucifixion really. Just pulling your leg.

NISUS

Oh . . . I see. Very good, very good. *(laughs forcedly)*
Oh jolly good . . . out of the door, line on the . . .

MR. CHEEKY

Yes . . . I know the way . . . out the door, line on the left, one cross each.

Meanwhile outside in the Forum a line of GUARDS *is struggling to keep back a surging crowd. A dozen men of the crack private guard have taken up strategic positions around the steps. Four* TRUMPETERS *appear on the top step and blow a fanfare.*

The CROWD *quietens.*

PILATE *and* BIGGUS *and the* CENTURION *appear on the balcony.*

PILATE

People of Jerusalem!

The CROWD *are grinning expectantly. The* CENTURION *closes his eyes, wiping sweat off his upper lip. The* CROWD *is generally in an ugly mood, quite threatening,*

but there is a hard core at the back of rather cheeky louts. The ringleader of these is called BOB HOSKINS.

PILATE

Wome is your Fwend!

A lot of the CROWD *giggle at this point. The* CENTURION *looks away, embarrassed.*

PILATE

To pwove our fwiendship, it is customawy at this time to welease a wong-doer fwom our pwisons.

A good laugh from the CROWD.

Whom would you have me welease?

CENTURION *bites his lip and looks heavenwards. He catches the eye of one* GUARD *who sniggers. The* CENTURION *freezes him with a look.*

BOB HOSKINS

Welease Wodger!

There are a few laughs and the CROWD *starts to pick this up immediately.*

CROWD

Yes! Welease Wodger! Welease Wodger! We want Wodger!

PILATE *turns to the* CENTURION *with an imperious air. The* CENTURION *bites his lip.*

PILATE

Very well, I shall welease . . . Wodger.

CENTURION

Er—we don't have a Rodger, sir.

PILATE

What?

CENTURION

We don't have anyone of that name, sir.

PILATE

Oh . . .
(he turns back to the crowd)
We have no Wodger.

ANOTHER

Welease Wodewick then.

CROWD

Yes, welease Wodewick.

PILATE *turns to* CENTURION.

PILATE

Why do they titter so?

CENTURION

Oh, it's just some Jewish joke, sir.

PILATE

(suspicions dawning)
Are they <u>wagging</u> me?

CENTURION

(hastily)
Oh <u>no</u>, sir.

BOB HOSKINS

How about weleasing Wodewick, then?

More laughter. PILATE *looks pleased and throws his arms wide in his benevolence.*

PILATE

Very well, I shall welease Wodewick.

CENTURION *looks increasingly pained.*

Er . . . we . . . don't have a Roderick either, sir.

PILATE

No Wodger? No Wodewick?
(he turns to the crowd)
Who is this Wodewick to whom you wefer?

BOB HOSKINS

He's a wobber!

More laughter.

ANOTHER

And a wapist!

More laughter.

ANOTHER

And a pick-pocket.

CROWD

No, ssh . . .

PILATE

Sounds a notowious cwiminal. Do we have anyone in our pwisons at all?

CENTURION

Oh, yes sir. We've got Samson, sir.

PILATE

Samson?

CENTURION

(as he unrolls a scroll)

Samson the Saducee strangler, sir. Silus the Syrian assassin, several seditious scribes from Caesarea . . .

BIGGUS *suddenly strides forward and grabs the scroll.*

145

(impressively)
Let me thpeak to them Ponthious.

CENTURION

(instinctively)
Oh, NO!

PILATE

Good idea, Biggus.

BIGGUS *strides forward and reads from the scroll.*

BIGGUS

THITizens! . . .

Inside the cells the crucifees are still being ticked off by
NISUS WETTUS. BRIAN *agitatedly awaits his turn.*

NISUS

Next. Crucifixion?

Yes.

NISUS

Good. Out of the door on the left, one cross each.
Thank you.

BRIAN

Excuse me!

NISUS

Just a minute if you don't mind. How many have
come through?

JAILER

What?

NISUS

How many have come through?

JAILER

What?

JAILER'S ASSISTANT

(who has been unlocking the manacles)
You'll have to spea . . . spea . . . spea . . .
speak up, sir. He's d . . . he's d . . . eaf as a p
. . . post, sir.

NISUS

(very loudly)
HOW . . . MANY . . . HAVE . . . COME
. . . THROUGH?

JAILER

(chuckles)
Heh. Heh.

NISUS

Oh dear.

JAILER'S ASSISTANT

(helpfully)
I make it ninety f . . . f . . . f . . . ninety f . . .
f . . . f . . . f . . . ninety f . . . ninety six, sir.

NISUS
Oh dear, it's such a senseless waste of human life, isn't it?

JAILER'S ASSISTANT
Not with these b . . . bastards, sir. C . . . c . . . c . . . cruci . . . cruci . . . crucifffff . . . crucifixion's too good for 'em sir.

NISUS
I don't think you can say it's too good for them. It's very nasty.

JAILER'S ASSISTANT
Not as n . . . n . . . n . . . nasty as something I just thought up.

JAILER
(suddenly, conspiratorially)
I know where to get it, it you want it.

NISUS
(confused)
What?

JAILER'S ASSISTANT
Don't worry about him. He's d . . . deaf and mad, sir.

NISUS
How did he get the job?

JAILER'S ASSISTANT
Bloody Pilate's pet!

MR. CHEEKY
Get a move on, Big Nose, people waiting to be crucified out here!
(laughs to himself)

BRIAN
Could I see a lawyer or someone?

NISUS

Do you have a lawyer?

BRIAN

No, but I am a Roman!

MR. CHEEKY

How about a retrial? We've got time!

ROMAN GUARD

(clouting him)

Shut up, you! Get in line!

MR. CHEEKY

I'm only sending him up.

ROMAN GUARD

Shut up!

MR. CHEEKY

Miserable bloody Romans—no sense of humour.

NISUS

I'm sorry, bit of a hurry. Could you go outside, line on the left, one cross each.

BRIAN *is hustled out, protesting.*

Back at the Forum, all is as before except that the entire CROWD *is prone on the ground, rolling around with their legs in the air and clutching their sides in unrestrained anarchic hilarity at what has obviously been a feast of verbal ineptitude.*

BIGGUS *is holding the scroll from which he has been reading. He looks mystified. He turns to the* CENTURION.

BIGGUS

Wath it thomething I thaid?

PILATE

Silence! This man commands a cwack legion! This man wanks as high as any man in Wome!

Renewed hilarity from the CROWD.

In the prison yard, 140 CRUCIFEES *are waiting to leave.* NISUS *addresses their massed ranks.*

NISUS

All right! Crucifixion party . . .

They look up wearily from under their burdens.

Morning. We <u>will</u> be on show as we go through the town, so let's not let the side down . . . let's keep in a good straight line . . . three lengths between you and the man in front . . . and a good steady pace . . . cross over your right shoulder, and if you keep your back tight up against the crossbeam, you'll be there before you know it.

PARVUS
Crucifixion party! . . . wait for it . . .
crucifixion party by the left . . . forrrward!

They shuffle off with groans and creaks.

As they move off there is a shout from inside the prison.
BEN *is upside down at the grille window.*

BEN
You lucky bastards! You lucky . . . jammy . . .
bastards!

JUDITH *now is running through the crowded streets.*
She reaches some steps and climbs up onto a roof.
Quickly, she opens a basket and releases a flock of
pigeons.

A very STRANGE MAN *is lying on a lonely hilltop.*

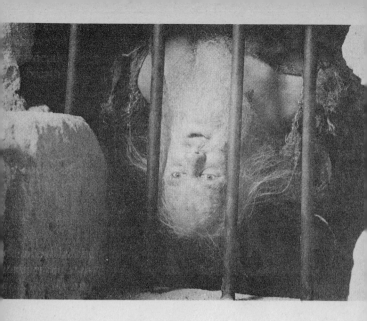

Suddenly he rouses himself, sits up and peers into the distance towards Jerusalem.

A flock of pigeons flies up against the sun.

Seeing this, the STRANGE MAN *rouses himself and does an extremely odd but elaborate dance.*

Further away, on an even lonelier hilltop, a pile of straw moves to reveal that it is in fact a MAN *dressed in straw. He watches the* STRANGE MAN'S *dance closely.*

> STRAW LOOK-OUT
>
> It is the sign!

Instantly OTTO *appears, with all his* MEN.

> OTTO
>
> The sign that is the sign?
>
> LOOK-OUT
>
> Yes!

OTTO

Men! Our time has come! Our Leader calls! Men forward!

The MEN *march into the wall and each other.*

OTTO

Oh my cock.

In the Jerusalem streets the procession of crosses trails through the city. They are going up a particularly steep road. Some are already beginning to crack. One man, ALFONSO, seems to be making particularly heavy weather of it. A rather saintly PASSER-BY comes up and quietly but authoritatively addresses him.

SAINTLY PASSER-BY

Let *me* shoulder your burden, brother.

He takes ALFONSO'S *cross.*

ALFONSO

Oh thank you . . .

He looks round . . . then races off.

SAINTLY PASSER-BY

Hey!

As the Saintly PASSER-BY *starts to put the cross down, the Centurion* PARVUS *hastens up.*

PARVUS

Hey what d'you think you're doing?

SAINTLY PASSER-BY

It's not *my* cross.

PARVUS

Shut up and get on with it.

MR. CHEEKY

Aha—he 'ad you there! That'll teach you a lesson—he got you all right.

Great amusement. The CRUCIFEES *are immensely cheered by this incident.*

There is a distant gale of laughter from the Forum. PILATE *is still at it.*

PILATE
I'm getting vewy angwy. Now I'll give you one more chance. Who would you have me welease?

MAN IN CROWD
Wobert!

BOB HOSKINS
No, we've done that one.

Suddenly JUDITH *appears breathless and agitated.*

JUDITH
Release Brian!

BOB HOSKINS

Oh, that's a good one. Yeth, welease Bwian!

The crowd's laughter is a bit forced by now, but they take up the chant 'Welease Bwian'.

PILATE

(blowing his top)·
Wight! That's it! I shall welease nobody!

The CROWD *'Ohs' with disappointment.*

CENTURION

Er! . . . We do have a Brian, sir!

PILATE

What?

CENTURION

You just sent him for crucifixion.

PILATE
(momentarily non-plussed)
Oh. Well, <u>welease</u> him, Centurion, stwaight away.

The CENTURION *dashes off as* PILATE *turns back to the crowd.*

PILATE
Very well. I shall welease Bwian!

The CRUCIFIXION PARTY *is now outside the city gates, heading towards Calvary. Some of the crosses are already up.* MR. CHEEKY *seems undeterred by this grim sight.*

PARVUS
Get a move on there!

MR. CHEEKY
Or what?

PARVUS

Or you'll be in trouble.

MR. CHEEKY

Oh dear! You mean I might have to give up being
crucified in the afternoons . . .

PARVUS

*(irritated at having his logical shortcoming
pointed out)*
Shut up!

MR. CHEEKY

That <u>would</u> be a blow . . . I wouldn't have
anything to do would I?

He gets a thump on top of his head from PARVUS.

MR. CHEEKY

Thank you. Bloody Romans.

Hot on the trail of BRIAN, *the tall* CENTURION *rushes down the steps into the empty cells. Only the* JAILER *and his* ASSISTANT *are left.*

CENTURION

Where have they gone?

JAILER

We've got lumps of it round the back.

CENTURION

What?

JAILER'S ASSISTANT

Oh don't worry about him. He's mm . . . mmm . . . mm . . . mad, sir.

CENTURION

Are they gone?

JAILER'S ASSISTANT

(gesturing strangely)

Oh n . . . n . . . n . . . n . . . n . . . n . . .

The CENTURION *gives up and races out.*

JAILER'S ASSISTANT

n . . . n . . . yes, sir. Anyway, go on with the story.

JAILER

Well, I knew that she'd never really fancied him so I thought to myself, ''What's she after then?''

Inside MANDY'S *kitchen, the* REVOLUTIONARIES *are still sitting round in mid-debate.*

REG

Right, that's the motion to get on with it carried with one abstention. I now propose we go without further ado. Could I have a seconder?

FRANCIS

No . . . let's just go.

158

Oh, all right . . .

They leave.

In the busy market streets, the CENTURION *and his* GUARDS *are elbowing people out of the way. The* CENTURION *pushes a* BEGGAR.

BEGGAR

Roman git!

CENTURION

Watch it, there's still some crosses left.

Indeed there are. One or two crosses are already up. A crucifix is being raised up efficiently into position by two or three ROMAN SOLDIERS. *They stand back. It is* BIG NOSE *on the cross.* PARVUS *is supervising.*

BIG NOSE

I'll get you for this, you bastard.

PARVUS

Oh yeah?

BIG NOSE

Oh yeah. Don't worry. I never forget a face.

PARVUS

No?

BIG NOSE

I'm going to definitely do you, old son.

PARVUS

Shut up, Jewish git.

BIG NOSE

Who are you calling Jew? I'm not a Jew. I'm a Samaritan.

An educated voice from the cross next door reveals MR. GREGORY; *already up on his cross, the same* SMALL BOY *still holds the tall umbrella over his head.*

A Samaritan? This is supposed to be a Jewish section.

PARVUS

It doesn't matter. You're all going to die in a day or two.

JEW

It may not matter to you Roman, but it certainly matters to us, doesn't it darling?

His WIFE, *nailed up on the cross next to him, nods in assent. People on the other crosses nod also. Murmurs of agreement.*

PHARISEE

Pharisees separate from Sadducees.

PARVUS

Alright. We'll soon settle this. Hands up those who don't want to be crucified here.

They strain to put their hands up.

PARVUS

Alright. Now just shut up the lot of you. Who's next?

The kindly man who shouldered ALFONSO'S *burden comes forward.*

PARVUS

Lie down on the wood.

SAINTLY PASSER-BY

It's not my cross.

PARVUS

What?

SAINTLY PASSER-BY

I'm only looking after it for somebody.

PARVUS
Just lie down, I haven't got all day.

SAINTLY PASSER-BY
Yes, of course. Look, I hate to make a fuss,
but . . .

PARVUS
Look, we've had a busy day . . . There's a
hundred and forty of you lot to get up, so let's just
cut the rabbit and get on with it.

GREGORY
Is <u>he</u> Jewish?

PARVUS
Belt up.

They push the cross on which the SAINTLY PASSER-BY
is roped up into the air and start fixing it in its socket.

SAINTLY PASSER-BY
Er . . . will you let me down if he comes back?

PARVUS
(airily)
Yes, yes—we'll let you down. Next!

BRIAN *is roughly grabbed and pushed forward.*

BRIAN
Look, you don't have to do this. You don't have
to take orders.

PARVUS
I <u>like</u> taking orders.

The REVOLUTIONARIES *meanwhile are marching
through the streets towards the city gate with grim
determination. Rather like a trade union delegation.
They are headed for Calvary, where* BRIAN'S *cross is
now raised up. We see for the moment his fear and
agony. A slight pause.*

MR. CHEEKY

See? Not so bad once yer up.

MR. CHEEKY is nodding away at BRIAN on the next cross.

MR. CHEEKY

You being rescued are you?

BRIAN

It's a bit late now, isn't it?

MR. CHEEKY

Nah—we've got a couple days up here—plenty of time—lots of people get rescued.

BRIAN

Oh.

MR. CHEEKY

My brother usually rescues me . . . if he can keep off the tail for more than twenty minutes . . . randy little bugger . . . he's up and down like the Assyrian Empire!

(laughs to himself)

'Ello, your family arrived then?

BRIAN

(with utter relief sees the REVOLUTIONARIES approaching)

Reg!

They group themselves under BRIAN'S cross, and REG steps forward.

REG

Hello, Sibling Brian.

BRIAN

Thank God you've come, Reg.

REG

Ah . . . now, I think I should point out in all
fairness, that we are not in fact the rescue committee.

(he unrolls a scroll)

However, I have been asked to read the following
prepared statement on behalf of the movement.

(he clears his throat)

"We, the People's Front of Judea brackets
Officials end brackets, do hereby convey our
sincere and heartfelt congratulations to you Brian
on this, the occasion of your martyrdom."

Nodding and murmurs of agreement from the others.
BRIAN *looks horrified.*

BRIAN

What?

"Your death will stand as a landmark in the continuing struggle to liberate the parent land once and for all from the hands of the Roman Imperialist aggressors, excluding those concerned with town drainage, roads, housing improvements, vintners, and all Romans who have contributed to the welfare of Jews of both sexes and hermaphrodites. Signed on behalf of the P.F.J. etc. . . . ."

(he lowers the scroll)

I'd just like to add on a personal note my own admiration for what you are doing for us at what must after all be, for you, Brian, a difficult time.

He rolls up the scroll. BRIAN *stares in disbelief.*

BRIAN

Reg . . . what are you going to . . .

REG

Goodbye, Brian, and thanks.

FRANCIS

Goodbye, Brian. Well done.

STAN

Very good, Brian, keep it up.

They regroup a little way away, turn and sing: "For He's A Jolly Good Fellow," then hurry away as the CENTURION *comes storming out of the city.*

CENTURION

Which one is Brian of Nazareth?

BRIAN

(still hurling abuse at the REVOLUTIONARIES*)*
You bastards!

CENTURION

I have an order here for his release.

BRIAN *is too busy abusing them to have heard.* MR. CHEEKY, *however, has not missed this.*

MR. CHEEKY

Oh, I'm Brian of Nazareth.

BRIAN

What?

MR. CHEEKY

I'm Brian of Nazareth.

CENTURION

Take him down then.

BRIAN

I'm Brian of Nazareth.

BIG NOSE
(catching on fast)
No, I'm Brian of Nazareth.

ANOTHER
I'm Brian.

MR. GREGORY
I'm Brian. And so's my wife.

ALL
I'm Brian! I'm Brian! I'm Brian!

MR. CHEEKY *is down off the cross.*

CENTURION
Release him.

MR. CHEEKY
No, only joking. I'm not really Brian.

He is carried away by the SOLDIERS.

MR. CHEEKY
I'm not Brian, I was having you on. Honestly, I
was just pulling your leg. I was taking the piss.

BRIAN
No, he's not Brian. I'm Brian.

ALL CRUCIFEES
I'm Brian, I'm Brian.

MR. CHEEKY
It's a joke. That's all. Put me back.

But he is dragged away. Suddenly PARVUS *looks up.*
He has heard something.

OTTO *and his* MEN *appear over the skyline.*

BRIAN
Otto!
(a new flicker of hope in his eyes)

OTTO
Men, charge!

They charge.

The ROMANS, *seeing this formidable army bearing down on them, finger their swords rather nervously and then break and run away back towards the city gate.*

BRIAN'S *face lights up with renewed hope as he sees* OTTO'S *army advancing at the double. The army arrives under the cross, swords held aloft. The* ROMANS *have all run away.*

OTTO

(to Brian)
Leader! We salute you. Men! Die for your cause!

With immaculate precision they all run themselves through, including OTTO.

OTTO

You see. Every man a hero. They died for their country.

BRIAN

You silly sods.

JUDITH *rushes up.*

JUDITH

Brian! Brian!

BRIAN

Judith!

JUDITH

Terrific! Great!

BRIAN

You mean I'm being released?

JUDITH

No, you're not, that's the point. Reg has explained it all to me and I think it's great what you are doing. Thank you, Brian. I'll . . . I'll never forget you.

She turns and hastens off.

Judith . . .

BRIAN *looks utterly depressed and in despair at this final desertion. Suddenly, a perky voice from the cross behind attempts to cheer him up.*

MR. FRISBEE III

Cheer up, Brian. You know what they say.
Some things in life are bad
They can really make you mad
Other things just make you swear and curse
When you're chewing on life's gristle
Don't grumble, give a whistle
And this'll help things turn out for the best . . .
And . . .
(the music slides into the song)
. . . always look on the bright side of life
(whistle)
Always look on the light side of life . . .
(whistle)
If life seems jolly rotten
There's something you've forgotten
And that's to laugh and smile and dance and sing,
When you're feeling in the dumps,
Don't be silly chumps
Just purse your lips and whistle—that's the thing.
And . . . always look on the bright side of
    life . . .
(whistle)
Come on.
(others start to join in)
Always look on the right side of life . . .
(whistle)
For life is quite absurd
And death's the final word
You must always face the curtain with a bow

Forget about your sin—give the audiences a grin
Enjoy it—it's your last chance anyhow.
So always look on the bright side of death
Just before you draw your terminal breath
Life's a piece of shit
When you look at it
Life's a laugh and death's a joke, it's true,
You'll see it's all a show,
Keep 'em laughing as you go
Just remember that the last laugh is on you.
And always look on the bright side of life . . .
(whistle)
Always look on the right side of life
(whistle)

Everyone is now singing away as the camera tracks back to reveal all the crosses in the late evening sunlight. The camera pans up and off towards the sky and the film fades.

THE END

Cheer up, you old bugger. Worse things happen at sea.
I mean what you got to lose? You come from nothing,
you're going back to nothing, what have you lost?
Nothing! Nothing will come from nothing. Know what
I mean? Cheer up.
Give us a grin. It's the end of the picture.
They'll never make their money back. I said to 'em,
"Bernie," I said, "they'll never make their money
back."

There are a lot more
where this one came from!

ORDER your FREE catalog of ACE paperbacks here. We have hundreds of inexpensive
books where this one came from priced from
75¢ to $2.50. Now you can read all the books
you have always wanted to at tremendous
savings. Order your *free* catalog of ACE
paperbacks now.

ACE BOOKS • P.O. Box 690, Rockville Centre, N.Y. 11571

Sharp Shooting
and
Rugged Adventure
from
America's Favorite
Western Writers

Winners of the SPUR and WESTERN HERITAGE AWARD

08383	**The Buffalo Runners** Fred Grove	$1.75
13905	**The Day The Cowboys Quit** Elmer Kelton	$1.25
29741	**Gold In California** Todhunter Ballard	$1.25
34270	**The Honyocker** Giles Lutz	$1.50
47082	**The Last Days of Wolf Garnett** Clifton Adams $1.75	
47491	**Law Man** Lee Leighton	$1.50
55123	**My Brother John** Herbert Purdum	$1.75
56025	**The Nameless Breed** Will C. Brown	$1.50
71153	**The Red Sabbath** Lewis B. Patten	$1.75
10230	**Sam Chance** Benjamin Capps	$1.25
82091	**Tragg's Choice** Clifton Adams	$1.75
82135	**The Trail To Ogallala** Benjamin Capps	$1.25
85903	**The Valdez Horses** Lee Hoffman	$1.75

Available wherever paperbacks are sold or use this coupon.

12J

Don't Miss these Ace Romance Bestsellers!

_____#75157 **SAVAGE SURRENDER** $1.95
*The million-copy bestseller by Natasha Peters,
author of Dangerous Obsession.*

_____#29802 **GOLD MOUNTAIN** $1.95

_____#88965 **WILD VALLEY** $1.95
*Two vivid and exciting novels by
Phoenix Island author, Charlotte Paul.*

_____#80040 **TENDER TORMENT** $1.95
*A sweeping romantic saga in the
Dangerous Obsession tradition.*

ROMANTIC SUSPENSE

Discover ACE's exciting new line of exotic romantic suspense novels by award-winning author Anne Worboys:

THE LION OF DELOS

RENDEZVOUS WITH FEAR

THE WAY OF THE TAMARISK

THE BARRANCOURT DESTINY

Coming soon:

HIGH HOSTAGE